Knights of The Ku Klux Klan

by

COL. WINFIELD JONES

Formerly of the Congressional Press Gallery

Published by
The Tocsin Publishers
511 West 113th Street
New York, N.Y.

TABLE OF CONTENTS

ILLUSTRATIONS

PUBLISHER'S NOTE

The author of the story of the Ku Klux Klan was for many years one of the ablest and most experienced of the Washington journalists. He conducted an extensive investigation of the Klan in the headquarters at Atlanta, Georgia, in Washington, nearly 20 years ago, and elsewhere throughout the country, and recently at Atlanta made a thorough search of its entire organization. His story is eminently fair, and describes only facts concerning the Ku Klux Klan, past and present.

The old Ku Klux Klan after the Civil War played a prominent part in Reconstruction days, one of the most important periods in the history of the United States. The story of the Klan is part of the history of the United States. These times are described from an historical standpoint, and make an interesting story of the efforts made in the South to recover political liberties that had been lost by the collapse of the Confederacy. Every important fact concerning the present Klan is described in this book.

The story is not in any sense an "expose" of the Ku Klux Klan, nor is it a defense, but an accurate description of this national organization, which is reported to be increasing its membership at the rate of more than 1,000 a day.

Colonel Jones is not a member of the Ku Klux Klan and was not born in the South, so that he made his investigation without any prejudice one way or the other, and solely from the viewpoint of the trained and impartial writer, bent on getting all the facts concerning the Klan, and writing the history in an accurate and interesting manner.

The author wishes to cordially thank Col. E. N. Sanctuary, of New York City, for kind and efficient assistance in publishing this book, in preparing the Mss. for publication, and in assisting in reading proofs and other matters connected with the work.

Colonel Sanctuary, a well known veteran of the World War I, and an accomplished writer and author, has been of the utmost assistance in preparing this book.

PREFACE

When I began to prepare to write the story of the Ku Klux Klan nearly twenty years ago, I knew nothing of the organization except what I had read in the newspapers, and I had not been interested in the subject. The task undertaken, however, I determined to get as many facts as possible about the Ku Klux Klan of the present and the past, and to write a concise, accurate history of the organization, new and old, without fear or favor, so that the truth could be laid before the public from an impartial standpoint. I had no interest in the subject other than to write facts. Therefore I first secured permission from Col. William Joseph Simmons, then Imperial Wizard of the Ku Klux Klan, at the organization's headquarters in Atlanta, to be given access to all the Klan's records, rituals, secret work, history correspondence, books, accounts, and historical documents, and in fact everything pertaining to the organization. This permission was obtained with great difficulty and only after repeated efforts, for the Imperial Wizard was reluctant to allow anyone to investigate the organization at headquarters.

I spent considerable time in the then Imperial Palace in Atlanta, and was given access to everything in that building. I feel sure that all the affairs of the organization were shown and that nothing was concealed. Once I had gained the confidence of the Imperial Wizard and the high officials they frankly and sincerely laid everything before me concerning the Order.

After I had secured everything at headquarters of the Klan and had made a thorough and painstaking investigation at this source, I ransacked the Congressional Library and other libraries for everything that had been printed concerning the old Ku Klux Klan, that originated soon after the Civil War. In this search I secured a large amount of extremely interesting information concerning Reconstruction days, including many original documents and letters describing episodes and occurrences of those stirring times when the "white horsemen" galloped over the South in their mission to restore the political and social rule of the Caucasian.

I also attended all the sessions of the second Congressional investigation in Washington, securing a copy of the testimony, and therefore, when I started to write the story I believed I had obtained most of the available information on the subject.

CHAPTER I

SOUTHERN CONDITIONS AFTER
THE CIVIL WAR

After Appomattox, when the immortal Grant said: "Let us have peace," the Confederacy lay prostrate in defeat. President Andrew Johnson, who succeeded the martyred Lincoln, meant well toward the conquered Southern States, but the Northern legislative policy between 1866 and 1872 did not carry out Johnson's views concerning reconstruction of the South. When the lamented Lincoln fell before the assassin Booth's bullet in Ford's theater, in the National Capital, Lincoln had already planned immediate reconstruction of the Southern States governments, and had planned, according to historians of that period, to readmit the conquered sister states into full fellowship with the victorious northern section. President Johnson fully intended to carry out this policy, but became involved in bitter disputes with Congress and the Republican majority in House and Senate, which repudiated the Lincoln policy, and decided to deal with the Southern States as conquered provinces and not as states.

Differences between President Johnson and the reconstruction Congress began when the President announced his policy toward the South, which was in practically every particular the Lincoln policy, but leaders of the Republican majority in House and Senate, embittered by the four years of war and the immense losses suffered by the Union armies, thought otherwise. The fight between Congress and President Johnson began when the President vetoed the Freedmen's Bureau Bill in February, 1866. A few months later Congress, in opposition to the administration, passed this bill over Johnson's veto. The Freedmen's Bureau, to be managed by the War Department, gave complete jurisdiction over practically everything pertaining to the recently freed slaves. It provided for the employment of Federal agents in all the southern counties, who might be either from civil life or from the army, and who had all the autocratic powers of military judges. The measure abolished ordinary processes of law, set aside the right of habeas corpus, destroyed the right of trial by jury, as well as the right of appeal from sentences. This law gave the Federal agents of the Freedmen's Bureau, who were soon swarming in every part of the South, more tyrannical and autocratic powers than were ever possessed by any Romanoff tyrant, Roman consul, Hitler, Mussolini, or Stalin. Under the bill, an agent of the Freedmen's Bureau, backed by Federal bayonets of negro troops, had for a time practically unlimited power over life and property in any county in the South where he set up his authority.

The Freedmen's Bureau Act was followed by three other measures in the 1866 Congress, all providing for "more efficient government of the rebel states." All of these measures were passed over President Johnson's veto, and the conflict between the Executive and Congress grew more bitter day by day. The measures divided ten of the defeated Southern States into five military districts, each in charge of an army officer who was endowed with absolute and arbitrary powers such as had hardly existed before in any country. President Johnson bitterly denounced these bills and flayed Congress in his veto messages. Naturally the breach between the President and Congress grew wider.

It cannot be denied that the bestowal of such tyrannical power upon military satraps in the South led to grave abuses in that section. Immense stealings and graft of all kinds, tyrannies, and persecutions of the defeated population occurred which finally culminated in a saturnalia of misgovernment which has hardly been paralleled in history. This condition afterwards was well recognized in the North and by former Union soldiers. Some Republican members of Congress were among the chief opponents of this policy.

Under these laws all men who had served in the Confederate Army, or aided in any way the Confederate States, were disfranchised and could not hold any state or Federal office. This condition continued almost universally in the South until 1872. The result was that the Southern white man had nothing whatever to say concerning his State or the Federal Government. He was governed by a horde of "carpet-baggers"[1] and "scala-

---

[1] Carpetbagger. A northern Federal appointee to assist in governing the South, under the Freedmen's Bureau. He was so-called because he usually came South with all his possessions in a carpetbag, which in those times was a common grip or valise used by nearly everybody.

11

wags"[2] of various kinds who invaded the South in large numbers after Appomattox, and after the Federal armies were largely disbanded. With the Caucasian race disfranchised, negro rule, led and directed by the white carpetbaggers from the North, followed as a matter of course.

The Congressional legislation provided that the five military districts into which the ten Southern States were organized should continue until these States held conventions and adopted new constitutions satisfactory to Congress. It was also required that their legislatures adopt the Fourteenth Amendment to the United States Constitution,[3] and arbitrary rule was to continue until the Fourteenth Amendment had been adopted by three-fourths of the States of the Union.

Under the urging of Senator Charles Sumner, of Massachusetts, a rabid foe of the Southern people, the Civil Rights Bill was then passed. This law authorized the Federal courts to compel admission of negroes to all public places, and made mandatory that negroes should serve on juries the same as whites. In 1883 the United States Supreme Court held the Civil Rights Bill unconstitutional.

---

[2] Scalawag. A native Southerner who turned against his own people and took the part of the North. Scalawags took employment with the Freedmen's Bureaus, and were universally detested by the Southern people, more so even than the Northern carpetbagger. Websters International Dictionary defines scalawag as a "scamp."

[3] See Appendix for Fourteenth Amendment.

12

CHAPTER II

REPUBLICANS VINDICTIVE TOWARD SOUTH

Republican members of Congress, who were responsible for the subjection under which the conquered Southern States groaned, set up the contention that conditions in the South required martial law. It is now generally realized in this enlightened age that such a procedure was unwarranted by conditions, and was largely the result of the bitter passions caused by the four years' struggle between the States. The American Constitution provides that a writ of *habeas corpus* shall not be suspended except in cases of rebellion or invasion. Every fair-minded man, after the lapse of the past more than three-fourths of a century, when the hatreds of the great war have been abated or been stilled, must acknowledge there was no excuse for claiming after the war ended that a state of rebellion existed in the South when the Confederate armies had surrendered and disbanded. Certainly there was no invasion of the South, but the right of *habeas corpus* was completely nullified by the military agents who governed the South with iron hands.

Most constitutional lawyers will acknowledge now that the reconstruction laws were unconstitutional, as well as wrong and vicious. Their application in the South held back the economic recovery of the Southern States for many years. With the perspective of seventy-eight years behind us we now see that these laws were wrong. Under these statutes practically the entire white population of the South was disfranchised. The former slaves, only a few of whom could read or write, constituted the entire electorate. The carpetbaggers, and the scalawags, some of whom were the scum of the earth, led this motley array of negroes and worked their will with them politically, at the same time that they plundered the white population of the South. It was not long before an era of oppression and corruption was in full swing that would have put to shame the most deplorable conditions in the history of any conquered country. So bad was the misgovernment in the South, and so corrupt the conditions prevailing under carpetbag rule, that many of the northern papers of that period printed scathing editorials against the agents of the Freedmen's Bureau and the Southern military government.

While the carpetbaggers and rascals of various kinds were misgoverning the South and plundering it, a few good men from the Northern States had immigrated to the South, and these men, many of them former Federal soldiers and officers, unhesitatingly took the part of the oppressed population. Their voices were continually heard in protest through communications to northern newspapers, concerning the saturnalia of robbery and misgovernment in the Southern States.

Veterans of the Federal armies and the Confederate armies in any Southern community in the United States, who are still alive, will personally corroborate these statements, (although there are few now) which do not begin to describe the terrible governmental conditions existing in the South for many years after the end of the Civil War.

In fact, the South was rapidly being reduced to a state of complete ruin by misgovernment of the carpetbaggers and their ignorant negro followers. The freed slaves, as a class, were good people. They had been, except in few cases, well treated and well taken care of by their owners, but in the mass they were illiterate, ignorant, and super-stitious, with a leavening of viciousness. They were as putty in the hands of their white leaders. It followed that the government of the Southern States, under such conditions, was undoubtedly one of the worst ever ex-perienced in the history of the world.

In every Southern State conditions were practically the same, but a few illustrations will suffice to give an idea of the misgovernment.

In South Carolina the land taxes in 1860 amounted to about $400,000. In 1871 they amounted to $2,000,000. The taxable values in that period shrank from $490,000,000 to $184,000,000. The taxes could not be paid. Lands were forfeited and either became waste places in enor-mous areas, or were handed over to the negroes. The state debt increased from $1,000,000 in 1867 to more than $30,000,000 in 1872.

In Mississippi nearly 7,000,000 acres of land were forfeited by the owners because the state taxes in 1874 had increased fourteenfold.

In a few years the public debt of Louisiana increased from approximately $6,000,000 to $50,000,000. The conditions that existed in Mississippi, South Carolina, and Louisiana prevailed in the other conquered Southern States.

While state misgovernment was so serious, the public affairs of cities, towns, villages, and counties were even in a worse condition, nearly all of them being bankrupt and owing public debts they could not pay and that were never paid. Many of the illegal debts contracted by states in this period were afterward repudiated when the whites ousted carpetbag rule and again secured control of state, county, and municipal governments.

As government conditions, including cities, towns, and villages, were as bad as possible the people suffered greatly. Freed from the labor of the plantations, hundreds of thousands of negroes left the land and crowded into the cities and towns. They were attracted by the hope of living on the bounty of the Government and securing financial support of the Freedmen's Bureau; but most of all they were drawn to the centers of population by the newly bestowed right of suffrage, and the hope of securing public offices which would make them the political superiors of their former masters. These negroes were promised "40 acres and a mule." They never got either.

As an illustration of the type of carpetbag and ignorant legislators during reconstruction days in the South, the South Carolina State Legislature of 1868-1872 contained 155 members. With hardly an exception they were either negroes or the lowest possible type of whites, and included a large number of carpetbaggers.

Twenty-two members could not read or write. Several were able to only write their names, and 41 signed official documents with an X-mark. Ninety-eight of the 155 members were negroes, and of this number 67 paid no taxes. None of the state officers, with the sole exception of the lieutenant governor, paid any taxes.

Negro militia companies were organized everywhere, and these were used as an instrument by agents of the Freedmen's Bureau and the military government to terrorize the people. The white men were not allowed to join the militia organizations and, whenever possible, they were deprived of arms. The agents of the Freedmen's Bureau and the military judges were bitterly prejudiced against the white population, favorably inclined to the negro, and as many of these officials were themselves ignorant, vicious, and of the lowest type there was practically no justice obtainable by the white man. Federal troops and the negro militia companies were quartered in the cities and towns and were the chief instruments to enforce the authority of the Freedmen's Bureau agents. White men and women were frequently arrested at the caprice of these agents and imprisoned for long periods without being brought before a court. The military commanders in the zones sometimes interfered at will with

17

the civil courts, and ordinary procedure of civil law was subject at any time to the whim of the Freedmen's Bureau agent or a military commander. In some cities civil officers were arbitrarily removed by military commanders, citizens were forbidden to assemble at any time, and even the highest judicial officers of a State Supreme Court were awed or menaced by armed men. A Louisiana Governor was summarily removed by order of a military commander. Military commanders on more than one occasion resisted court decrees and forced judges to revoke sentences of their courts. Criminals were forcibly taken from peace officers by negro militia officers and set free. The white man was an object of insult, and women were never safe from the vilest crimes. Newspapers were suppressed and public lectures forbidden. The Federal soldiers, including the negro militia, managed elections and took charge of the ballot boxes. Citizens who had perpetrated no crimes were seized without authority of law and incarcerated in "bull pens" where formerly negro criminals had been confined.

Of course, among the horde of agents of the Freedmen's Bureau and among the military officers were men of honesty and high character, but they were in the hopeless minority, and while in their jurisdictions comparatively good government prevailed and justice was administered fairly, these were isolated instances. Some of these honest and capable officers, though few in numbers, did not fail to vigorously protest against deplorable conditions in the South whenever they returned to the North, and gradually there began to percolate through the North a feeling that all was not well in the South.

18

Inflamed by the losses and perils of the four-year struggle, irritated by the disorganized condition of the North at the end of the Civil War, and swollen with the elation of victory, the Republican Congress of that period had very little respect for the President or even the Supreme Court of the United States. Between 1864 and 1876 Congress treated the United States Supreme Court with the utmost contempt. When President Johnson attempted to remove Secretary of War Stanton under the authority of the "tenure of office act," Congress contemptuously rejected the proposition and attempted to impeach Mr. Johnson. The fact is, in this period of our history, Congress had usurped the duties of the President, the judicial branches of government, and was unchecked by any authority.

The Constitution did not specify a way to restore government in the Southern States, and Congress believed that in view of this omission the law-making function for the conquered states fell to it. President Johnson believed that he had authority, as commander-in-chief of the army and navy, the Constitution failing to provide a method of restoration by the establishment of military law. The President, therefore, began actual reconstruction, evidently with the best motives, but Congress overthrew all of his plans and began reconstruction legislation of its own. Many Northern members of Congress believed that special and vigorous laws should be passed to govern the South, as they feared that the former slaves could not defend themselves or secure any of their rights against the intelligence and courage of the Southern white men.

Lincoln in '63, had announced his plan of reconstruction in which he offered pardon to all conquered citizens of the South, with a few exceptions, if they would swear loyalty to the Union and agree to abide by the laws and proclamations respecting slavery. The martyred President hoped that the white population in the South would take the oath, but his assassination completely upset his plans. Had the great President lived there would have been a peaceful and speedy reconstruction of the South. Radical Northern leaders thought President Lincoln too mild toward the conquered South, but from contemporary newspapers it is known that Lincoln's plan met the approval of the North, where there was little, if any, desire to punish the South, particularly among the returned Union soldiers.

During consideration by Congress of reconstruction methods various theories of the status of the conquered states appeared.

The first was that the Southern States only needed to accept the fact of the abolition of slavery, agree to the reestablishment of Federal authority, and resume their former places in the Union.

President Johnson held that when he granted amnesty to the Southern officials and former Confederate commanders the people of the South could reform their state governments and resume their places in the Union. Some of the hot-headed Northern congressmen believed that the rebels had forfeited their constitutional rights and therefore the Federal Government, represented by

Congress, had the power to govern the South as it pleased and to dictate the terms on which the defeated states could be readmitted to the Union. Another theory was that the war had caused the states to cease to exist as states, that they were now merely conquered provinces, and that Congress might do as it would with the people and their territory. Out of these theories grew the Freedmen's Bureau Bill and the other reconstruction acts.

The South lay prostrate and groaned in her chains. Southern white men believed that something had to be done immediately, or all culture would perish south of the Ohio River, to be succeeded by a mongrel civilization which would absorb or extinguish the old Anglo-Saxon race and blood. The conditions were deplorable and the white men were desperate. Armed resistance and another rebellion were out of the question, though writers of that period are practically unanimous in the opinion that if the conditions had continued longer without check guerrilla warfare would have begun everywhere in the South. A remedy against carpetbag domination and negro rule had to be found. It was found by the Southern white man in the secret organization known as the Ku Klux Klan.

CHAPTER III

ORGANIZATION OF THE KU KLUX KLAN

Like many other great organizations, the Ku Klux Klan started with a small beginning.

The original Ku Klux Klan was organized May 6, 1866, in the town of Pulaski, Tennessee. Life was dull in Pulaski, Tennessee, in 1866. At that time it was a mere village. The writer visited Pulaski, which is now a thriving town of about 3,800 people. A few of the first Ku Kluxers are still alive. In that month and year, six young men, some of whom were former Confederate soldiers, happened to meet together in an office one night, and as time hung heavy on their hands in such a small village as Pulaski, one of these young men (whose name has not been preserved to posterity) suggested that they organize a society for the purpose of mutual entertainment. Old residents of Pulaski differ on whether the meeting was held in the office of a young lawyer of the town, or in the office of a physician over a drug store, or whether it was held in an abandoned brick house. At any rate the young men held the meeting and decided to organize the new society. Probably nothing was further from their thoughts when they met that night than that the organization was destined to grow into what it afterward became.

At this meeting one of the young men suggested they call the new society "Kuklos," from the Greek word "Kuklos," meaning "circle," and another young man suggested an improvement on that name, so that by unanimous consent they decided to call the new organization "Ku Klux." Someone then suggested that the word "Klan" be added in order to make an alliterative name. Stories published later to the effect that the Ku Klux Klan had derived its name from the ancient Scottish clans are erroneous. This idea probably started from the fact that part of the paraphernalia in the ritual work of the Ku Klux Klan includes a fiery cross. The Scottish clans, when they summoned their men to war, sent a messenger around who bore a blazing cross, and from this fact writers concerning the Ku Klux Klan fell into the error that the Klan's fiery cross originated with the Scottish cross.

Another meeting was held by the young men, and the organization was perfected as far as it then went. Various devices were invoked to arouse the curiosity of the public and surround the organization with an atmosphere of mystery. An oath was devised which bound each member to absolute secrecy regarding anything pertaining to the Klan, and he also swore that he would never tell he was a member of the Ku Klux, nor would he ever disclose the name of any other member.

At the third meeting of the new organization it was decided to have a regalia consisting of a long white robe, with a white mask, and a very tall hat made of white pasteboard with a projecting spike in the crown. The officers of the original organization of the young men's society included a "Grand Cyclops," who was the president or presiding officer; a "Grand Turk," who was the marshal or master of ceremonies. The "Grand Exchequer" was the treasurer. There were two Lictors who were the inner and outer guards on the meeting place, which was called the "Den." The meetings there were always held at night in an old brick house, which had been deserted for some years, on the outskirts of Pulaski.

For a long time the only business conducted by the parent Ku Klux Klan was the initiation of new members, and the only purpose of the organization then was to have an enjoyable time and to mystify the inhabitants of Pulaski.

Newspapers in Giles County, in which Pulaski is located, began to discuss the new organization, and within a few months the membership increased. It was not very long before other "Dens" were organized throughout Giles County. Red lights and horseplay used at initiations, which were often conducted in graveyards and deserted houses, soon began to be noticed by the negro population. It was a favorite joke for the white-robed Ku Kluxers to make solitary patrols along the roads of the county, and the ignorant and superstitious negroes, as well as some of the white people, began to discuss the mystery and apparent menace of the white riders. A story got abroad among the ignorant negroes that the Ku Kluxers were the ghosts of Confederate soldiers, and it was not long before the negroes were afraid to venture out of their cabins at night.

It is difficult to imagine the dark superstition and universal ignorance of the negro race in the South during slavery times and for years afterward. The Ku Kluxers seemed to the ignorant negroes to have some connection with their beliefs of various kinds in the powers of Satan, and the tales spread until soon it was difficult to induce any negro to leave his home after dark. The Pulaski Ku Klux and the other organizations throughout Giles County which had sprung from the parent organization had no intention of terrorizing the negro population, which in Tennessee in that year was comparatively peaceful.

It was not very long until the prime movers in the Ku Klux Klan were aware that their actions and mysterious movements exercised a profound impression on the negro population and "poor white trash." It then occurred to them that a power had been placed in their hands that could be used to keep the recently freed negroes peaceful and law abiding, and they were not slow to take advantage of this fact.

In 1867 the rapidity with which the Ku Klux Klan spread throughout the State of Tennessee was little short of marvelous. Scores of "Dens" were inaugurated and the Order soon numbered many thousands in the old Volunteer State. From Tennessee the movement spread to Mississippi and Alabama with great rapidity. From these states it extended to all of the Southern States and penetrated the South as far as parts of Texas. There were in all probably 4,000 to 5,000 "Dens" in the South, but each "Den" was an individual organization, answer-

Burning the Fiery Cross on Stone Mountain

able to itself alone. There was no central organization or federation of the "Dens."

In the early part of 1867 some of the Pulaski leaders sent out a request to all the "Dens" of which they had knowledge to send delegates from each "Den" to a convention to be held in Nashville, Tennessee. These delegates met secretly in Nashville in the spring of 1867 and organized a national organization, which, however, included only the Southern States. It was here that the name of "Invisible Empire" originated, and the "Invisible Empire" meant the whole territory in which the Klans existed. The National Convention divided the "Invisible Empire" into Dominions, which corresponded to Congressional Districts, and each Dominion was divided into Provinces, each Province consisting of a county, in which county or Province were "Dens," or the local Klans.

The National Convention elected a head of the Order who was called the "Grand Wizard." Gen. Nathan Bedford Forrest, celebrated Confederate cavalry leader, whose home was in Memphis, Tennessee, was the first "Grand Wizard." It is an interesting coincidence that his son, the late Nathan Bedford Forrest, of Atlanta, Georgia, was once the business manager of Lanier University in Atlanta, which was owned by the present Ku Klux Klan. The chief judicial officer of the original Ku Klux Klan was the celebrated Gen. Albert Pike, of Arkansas, father of Scottish Rite Masonry in the United States. Many former Confederate officers of high rank were among its chief officers. Gen. John B. Gordon of Georgia, Gen. W. J. Hardee of Alabama, Gen. Wade Hampton of South

Carolina, and Senator A. H. Colquitt of Georgia were among these men.

The ruler of the dominion or congressional district was the "Grand Titan," that of the province or a county was called a "Grand Giant," and the head of a "Den" was denominated a "Grand Cyclops."

It is to be regretted from an historical standpoint that the names of the men who attended the secret convention where the Ku Klux Klan really sprang into being are not obtainable, but even newspapers in Nashville at that time did not know the convention was held, and records of the meeting have disappeared, as diligent search in the headquarters of the Ku Klux Klan in Atlanta and elsewhere failed to disclose these documents.

The National Convention gave a tremendous impetus to the organization, and by the end of 1868 the Klans practically dominated many large portions of the South. Of its total membership we have no knowledge at this time, but it must have been very large, several hundred thousand at least. One writer of the time declares that the Klan numbered at the crest of its power and influence more than 600,000 men, many of whom were former Confederate soldiers and officers. Some of the "Grand Titans" and "Grand Giants" had held high rank in the Confederate army.

There is one striking fact in an investigation of the documents of the old Ku Klux Klan, and that is the oath taken by every Klansman always included an obligation to support the Constitution of the United States, the cause

28

of humanity and justice, and there was a special obligation to protect all widows and orphans.

While the supreme authority of the "Invisible Empire" was vested in the "Grand Wizard," just as it is vested today in the "Imperial Wizard" of the modern Klan, James A. Colescott, and the chief office was held for life, or resignation, the authority of the "Grand Wizard" was very loosely held, because of the disturbed condition surrunding communications in the South at that time. The writer has been told by several of the old Ku Kluxers that the "Grand Wizard," the "Grand Titans," and the "Grand Giants" always sent their orders to the "Grand Cyclops" of a "Den" by mounted messenger, and nothing was ever entrusted to the mails. Then, too, owing to the rather loose organization of the "Invisible Empire" and the difficulty of communication except by messenger, the "Grand Cyclops" and commander of a "Den" and his assistants were practically a law unto themselves, and all activities in their neighborhoods or counties usually originated in the "Den."

CHAPTER IV

DECLARATION OF FIRST KLANSMEN

While the records of the Nashville secret convention are lost, there is in existence a statement of the chief principles of the Order at that time which contains the following:

"We recognize our relation to the United States Government, the supremacy of the Constitution, the Constitutional laws thereof, and the Union of the States thereunder."

The special objects of the Order were set out as follows:

"1. To protect the weak, the innocent, and the defenseless from the indignities, wrongs, and outrages of the lawless, the violent, and the brutal; to relieve the injured and the oppressed; to succor the suffering and unfortunate, and especially the widows and orphans of Confederate soldiers.

"2. To protect and defend the Constitution of the United States and laws passed in conformity thereto, and to protect the states and people thereof from all invasion from any source whatever.

"3. To aid and assist in the execution of all Constitutional laws, and to protect the people from unlawful seizure, and from trial except by their peers in conformity with the laws of the land."

Fleming's "Documentary History of Reconstruction" gives the following declaration of the Nashville convention:

"This organization shall be styled and denominated the Order of the Ku Klux Klan.

"We, the Order of the Ku Klux Klan, reverentially acknowledge the majesty and supremacy of the Divine Being, and recognize the goodness and providence of the same. And we recognize our relation to the United States Government, the supremacy of the Constitution, the Constitutional Laws thereof, and the Union of States thereunder.

"This is an insitution of Chivalry, Humanity, Mercy, and Patriotism; embodying in its genius and its principles all that is chivalric in conduct, noble in sentiment, generous in manhood, and patriotic in purpose; its peculiar objects being:

"First: To protect the weak, the innocent, and the defenseless, from the indignities, wrongs, and outrages of the lawless, the violent, and the brutal; to relieve the injured and oppressed; to succor the suffering and unfortunate, and especially the widows and orphans of Confederate soldiers.

"Second: To protect and defend the Constitution of the United States, and all laws passed in conformity thereto, and to protect the States and the people thereof from all invasion from any source whatever.

"Third: To aid and assist in the execution of all Constitutional laws, and to protect the people from unlawful seizure, and from trial except by their peers in conformity to the laws of the land.

"Section 1. The officers of this Order shall consist of a Grand Wizard of the Empire, and his ten Genii; a Grand Dragon of the Realm, and his eight Hydras; a Grand Titan of the Dominion, and his six Furies; a Grand Giant of the Province, and his four Goblins; a Grand Cyclops of the Den, and his two Night-hawks; a Grand Magi, a Grand Monk, a Grand Scribe, a Grand Exchequer, a Grand Turk, and a Grand Sentinel.

"Section 2. The body politic of this Order shall be known and designated as 'Ghouls.'

"Section 3. The territory embraced within the jurisdiction of this Order shall be coterminous with the States of Maryland, Virginia, North Carolina, South Carolina, Georgia, Florida, Alabama, Mississippi, Louisiana, Texas, Arkansas, Missouri, Kentucky and Tennessee; all combined constituting the Empire.

"Section 4. The Empire shall be divided into four departments the first to be styled the Realm, and coterminous with the boundaries of the several states; the second to be styled the Dominion, and to be coterminous with such counties as the Grand Dragons of the several Realms may assign to the charge of the Grand Titan. The third to be styled the Province, and to be coterminous with the several counties; provided, the Grand Titan may, when he deems it necessary, assign two Grand Giants to one Province, prescribing, at the same time, the jurisdiction of each. The fourth department to be styled the Den, and shall embrace such part of a Province as the Grand Giant shall assign to the charge of a Grand Cyclops."

32

The following questions were asked of candidates for membership:

"1st. Have you ever been rejected, upon application for membership in the Ku Klux Klan, or have you ever been expelled from the same?

"2d. Are you now, or have you ever been, a member of the Radical Republican party, or either of the organizations known as the 'Loyal League' and the 'Grand Army of the Republic'?

"3d. Are you opposed to the principles and policy of the Radical party, and to the Loyal League, and the Grand Army of the Republic, so far as you are informed of the character and purpose of those organizations?

"4th. Did you belong to the Federal army during the late war, and fight against the South during the existence of the same?

"5th. Are you opposed to negro equality, both social and political?

"6th. Are you in favor of a white man's government in this country?

"7th. Are you in favor of Constitutional liberty, and a government of equitable laws instead of a government of violence and oppression?

"8th. Are you in favor of maintaining the Constitutional rights of the South?

"9th. Are you in favor of re-enfranchisement and emancipation of the white men of the South, and the restitution of the Southern people to all their rights, alike proprietary, civil, and political?

"10th. Do you believe in the inalienable rights of self-preservation of the people against the exercise of arbitrary and unlicensed power?"

While the candidate was being initiated with impressive rites, in the presence of the flaming cross, and surrounded by the white robed brotherhod of the "Den," the following charge was administered:

"You have been initiated into one of the most important Orders which has ever been established on this continent: an Order which, if its principles are faithfully observed and its objects diligently carried out, is destined to regenerate our unfortunate country and to relieve the White Race from the humiliating condition to which it has lately been reduced in this Republic.

"Our main and fundamental object is the MAINTENANCE OF THE SUPREMACY OF THE WHITE RACE in this Republic. History and Physiology teach us that we belong to a race which nature has endowed with an evident superiority over all other races, and that the Maker, in thus elevating us above the common standard of human creation, has intended to give us over inferior races a dominion from which no human laws can permanently derogate. The experience of ages demonstrate that, from the origin of the world, this dominion has always remained in the hands of the Caucasian Race; whilst all the other races have constantly occupied a subordinate and secondary position; a fact which triumphantly confirms this great law of nature. And it is a remarkable fact that as a race of men is more remote from the Caucasian and

34

approaches nearer to the black African, the more fatally that stamp of inferiority is affixed to its sons, and irrevocably dooms them to eternal imperfectibility and degradation.

"Convinced that we are of these elements of natural ethics, we know, besides, that the government of our Republic was established by white men, for white men alone and that it never was in contemplation of its founders that it should fall into the hands of an inferior and degraded race. We hold, therefore, that any attempt to wrest from the white race the management of its affairs in order to transfer it to the control of the black population, is an invasion of the sacred prerogatives vouchsafed to us by the Constitution, and a violation of the laws established by God himself; that such encroachments are subversive of the established institutions of our Republic, and that no individual of the white race can submit to them without humiliation and shame.

"As an essential condition of success, this Order proscribes absolutely all social equality between the races. If we were to admit persons of African race on the same level with ourselves, a state of personal relations would follow which would unavoidably lead to political equality; for it would be a virtual recognition of status, after which we could not consistently deny them an equal share in the administration of our public affairs. The man who is good enough to be our familiar companion is good enough also to participate in our political government; and if we were to grant the one there could be no good reason for us not to concede the other of these two privileges.

"There is another reason, Brothers, for which we condemn this social equality. Its toleration would soon be a fruitful source of intermarriages between individuals of the two races; and the result of this miscegenation would be gradual amalgamation and the production of a degenerate and bastard offspring, which would soon populate these States with a degraded and ignoble population and unfitted to support a great and powerful country. We must maintain the purity of the white blood, if we would preserve for it that natural superiority with which God has ennobled it.

"To avoid these evils, therefore, we take the obligation TO OBSERVE A MARKED DISTINCTION BETWEEN THE TWO RACES.

"Our statutes make us bound to respect sedulously the rights of the colored inhabitants of this Republic, and in every instance, to give them whatever lawfully belongs to them. It is an act of simple justice not to deny them any of the privileges to which they are legitimately entitled; and we cannot better show the inherent superiority of our race than by dealing with them in that spirit of firmness, liberality and impartiality which characterizes all superior organizations. Besides, it would be ungenerous for us to exercise certain rights, without conceding to them, at the same time, the fullest measure of those which we recognize as theirs; and a fair construction of a white man's duty towards them would be, not only to respect and observe their acknowledged rights, but also to see that these are respected and observed by others.

"From the brief explanation whch I have just given you, you must have satisfied yourselves that our Association is not a political party, and has no connection with any of the organized parties of the day. Nor will it lend itself to the personal advancement of individuals, or listen to the cravings of any partisan spirit. It was organized in order to carry out certain great principles, from which it must never swerve by favoring private ambitions and political aspirations: These, as well as all sentiments of private enmity, animosity and other personal feelings, we must leave at the door before we enter this Council. You may meet here, congregated together, men who belong to all the political organizations which now divide, or may divide this country."

No distinction was made in the original Klan concerning Jews and Catholics. Negroes, of course, were not admitted to membership in the old Klan. Many Jews and Catholics, former Confederate soldiers, belonged to the original Klan.

CHAPTER V

WHY THE FIRST KU KLUX KLAN GREW

One of the causes of the immense growth of the Ku Klux Klan throughout the South was the organization of "Union Leagues." Union Leagues were organized everywhere throughout the South and they were composed principally of negroes with a sprinkling of white officials. The Union Leagues had the avowed purpose to politically dominate the South. History repeated itself according to the ancient dictum, for until recently there was in process of organization in the United States, with headquarters in Washington, D. C., the Anti-Ku Klux Klan Society, whose officers were negroes and its chief advisers certain members of Congress from the Northern States, only with this difference—that whereas one of the principal reasons for organization and spread of the Ku Klux Klan after the secret Nasville Convention was the Union Leagues throughout the South, organization of the Anti-Ku Klux Klan Society, followed the last Congressional investigational of the present Ku Klux Klan. Whenever a powerful organization has arisen in any country, nearly always an opposition society soon appears.

After 1868 there were rivals of the Ku Klux Klan in the South. These included "Knights of the White Camelia," for a time a powerful federated society having its largest membership in Louisiana. The "Constitutional Union Guards," the "White Brotherhood," the "Council of Safety," the " '76 Association," and the "Pale Faces" were others. After 1868 all these organizations, including the Ku Klux Klan, were societies of armed whites actually struggling for control of government in the South and for white supremacy. Later were organized the "White Line of Mississippi," the "White League" of Louisiana, and the "Rifle Clubs" of South Carolina. These were all manifestations of the Ku Klux spirit which had at its roots the determination of the white man to control government in the South, and to wrest that control from negroes and carpetbaggers.

All these secret societies, but more particularly the Ku Klux Klan, operated, one might say, on a local basis. That is, a Ku Klux "Den" of Pulaski, Tennessee, or one anywhere else, decided upon what it should do with very little reference to the authority of the Grand Wizard. These activities were, however, local, as the men of the local Klan were better able to judge of local affairs. In all other matters the authority of the Grand Wizard was always recognized. Activities of the "Den" varied according to circumstances. Some were purely protective in purpose and existed only to check the excesses of the newly freed blacks, who, suddenly released from slavery, perpetrated serious crimes and misdemeanors. Those punished or intimidated by the Klansmen often became, if not good citizens, at least quiet negroes. Some of the "Dens" expelled vicious county and town public officials.

Some acted as regulators of the morals of the public, others worked to keep the negroes from securing land, and the chief object of other "Dens" was to drive the blacks away from the plantations where they were born, and upon which they had been placed by agents of the Freedmen's Bureau.

It cannot be denied that the work of the Ku Kluxers was both good and bad. They kept the negro quiet, made life and property safe, protected womanhood, stopped incendiarism, and in a great many sections terrorized the agents of the Freedmen's Bureau, many of whom would have become, without some sort of check, the most despicable local tyrants. The Klan put to death a few of the worst of the Federal agents, and ran others out of the South.

The Ku Klux Klan led the fight in the Southern States for the white population to secure control of government from the blacks and the carpetbaggers. On the other hand, much evil sprang from the activities of the Ku Klux Klan. Lawless men made use of the organization as a cloak to cover their misdeeds of various kinds, and as a vehicle for taking vengeance on private enemies.

The real explanation of these disordered times was that the laws were bad and viciously administered. Therefore the people as a mass were aroused to secure self-protection.

As an illustration of conditions which existed in the old Ku Klux days, and the disorder which was prevalent in practically every community in the South, we find that in Orange County, North Carolina, three persons were hung for burning barns, one was hung for theft, and another for committing rape. Whether or not the local Ku Klux "Den" acted as the instrument of justice was never known, but at that time it was certain that the carpetbag officials were unable or unwilling to control criminals. At that date in North Carolina the carpetbaggers and negroes had three secret organizations of their own—the "Union League," the "Red Strings," and the "Heroes of America."

Conditions such as are described in this story are lamentable but true. In 1870 and 1871 George Sumners, an Englishman, traveled throughout the South. Sumners was an impartial foreign observer of conditions in the South. Here is what he said concerning a general survey that he made of ten of the Southern States:

"The white people in the South at the close of the war were alarmed, not so much by the threatened confiscation of their property by the Federal Government, as by more present dangers of life and property, virtue and honor, raising from the social anarchy around them. The negroes were disorderly. Many of them would not settle down to labor on any terms, but roamed about with arms in their hands and hunger in their bellies, and the governing power, with the usual blind determination of a victorious party, was thinking only all the while of every device of suffrage and reconstruction by which the 'freedmen' might be strengthened and made, under Northern dictation, the ruling power in the country. Agitators of the loosest fiber came down among the towns and plantations, and organizing a Union League, held midnight meetings with the negroes in the woods, and went about uttering sentiments which, to say the least, in all circumstances were antisocial and destructive. Crimes and outrages increased. The law, which must be always more or less weak in thinly populated countries, was all but powerless, and the new governments in the South were unable to repress disorders or to spread a general sense of security throughout the community. A real terror reigned for a time among the white people, and in this situation the Ku Klux started into being. It was one of those secret organizations which spring up in disordered states of society, when the bonds of law and government are all but dissolved, and when no confidence is felt in the regular administration of justice. But the power with which the Ku Klux moved in many parts of the South, the knowledge it displayed of all that was going on, the fidelity with which its secret was kept, and the complacency with which it was regarded by the general community, gave this mysterious body a prominence and importance seldom attained by such illegal associations. Nearly every respectable man in the Southern States was not only disfranchised, but under fear of arrest or confiscation; the old foundations of authority were utterly razed before any new ones had yet been laid, and in the dark and benighted interval the remains of the Confederate armies swept, after a long and heroic day of fair fight, from the field—flitted before the eyes of the people in this weird and midnight shape of a 'Ku Klux Klan.' "

JAMES A. COLESCOTT
Present and fourth Imperial Wizard — Knights of the Ku
Klux Klan.

43

CHAPTER VI

WORK OF THE FIRST KU KLUX KLAN

An air of mystery and secrecy always surrounded the operations of a local "Den" of the Ku Klux Klan. No person not a member of the "Den" ever knew when the "Den" met, and in some "Dens" the members did not know each other. Only the "Grand Cyclops" and his assistants had the membership roll, and knew by name and usually by sight the whole local membership.

Fair-minded investigators agree that in reconstruction days the Ku Klux Klan performed many acts of violence and intimidation, but in a search of the old records and newspapers of those times it has been impossible to find any instance where the Ku Klux Klan, regularly organized as a local "Den," maltreated or molested in any way peaceful and quiet citizens, either white or black. The activities of the white-clad riders were invariably directed against bad white men and disorderly negroes. In a large majority of cases the work of the Klan did not involve personal violence, and in most instances the mere knowledge of the fact that the Ku Kluxers were organized in any neighborhood was sufficient to make that section law-abiding, quiet, and orderly.

Often written warnings were sent to objectionable men among the white and black population, and these communications usually were pinned at night upon the doors of the houses of those who were warned. A rude scrawl, decorated with skull and cross bones, and signed Ku Klux Klan, was usually sufficient to cause the objectionable white or black to speedily mend his ways. If he persisted in being obnoxious to the neighborhood, a solitary Ku Kluxer, robed in white, would rap at his door at night and personaly serve notice on him that if he persisted in his evil ways the Klan would take strong measures. Only a few acts of violence were perpetrated in places where the local "Dens" were well organized, and any visitations from the Klan which involved bodily punishment were nearly always, it must be acknowledged, deserved by the victim, provided the local law had ignored his misdeeds. The times were extraordinarily disorderly, and while the Ku Klux Klan operated in defiance of organized law, the organized law itself, in many sections, was powerless or ineffective. Under such conditions it was natural that some force for law and order, such as the Ku Klux Klan, existed.

In many instances where Union Leagues held meetings at night, or where unruly or disorderly negroes gathered in considerable numbers, the white-clad horsemen silently appeared on the roads leading to the meeting places, and usually this warning was sufficient without any act of violence.

The superstitious or criminally inclined negroes and whites were watched closely everywhere, and sometimes a "Den" would divide itself into squads and ride all night, appearing in widely separate sections of the country, where their mere appearance was sufficient to intimidate the unruly whites and the superstitious negroes. It was a favorite warning of the Ku Kluxers to have one of their number appear at the cabin of a marked negro at night and ask for a drink of water. The Klansman would apparently drink a whole bucket of water, the fluid being contained in some receptacle, rubber bag or canteen, concealed on his person, and after the enormous draft had been swallowed, he would remark to the frightened negro that "it was the first drink he had received since he had been killed at the Battle of Shiloh." People who have spent any time in the South, even in these times, can readily understand how the extremely superstitious negro could be frightened, no matter how unreasonable this incident would seem.

In other cases, where warnings were not sufficient to curb undesirable characters, particularly drunkards, disorderly persons, and horse and cattle thieves, many of them whites, more strenuous methods were adopted. The victim would be seized at night and taken to the woods or a nearby corn field and soundly beaten. He would then be released with the injunction to "go and sin no more," and usually one visitation of this kind was sufficient to accomplish the purpose sought. Where more serious crimes were committed, such as murder, robbery, or rape, the culprit was taken at night and hung to a tree on the public highway, or if not executed in this manner he was shot.

In all the history of the operation of the Ku Klux Klan in the old South there is not one recorded instance, as far as the writer can find, where any woman, white or black, was molested by the Klansmen.

Occasionally it occurred that the carpetbag officials of a county or an agent of the Freedmen's Bureau were obnoxious to the population. The Klan would serve notice to depart from the neighborhood, and in most instances these men left between suns. If they did not heed the warnings they were seized and thrashed, and, in some isolated cases, hung or shot.

On more than one occasion the carpetbag officials, backed by the bayonets of the negro militia, refused to heed the warnings, and a pitched battle, usually at night, would occur, in which the Ku Kluxers nearly always came off victorious. Many were killed or wounded on both sides in these sanguinary affrays.

The Klan paid particular attention to righting wrongs of widows and orphans. Any person who oppressed the defenseless was certain to receive a warning from the Klan, and unless he speedily corrected his ways a visitation of the night riders would occur which gave him considerable bodily pain and, in extreme cases, cost his life.

The Klan also marked with its all-seeing eye persons who endeavored to incite the blacks against the whites, and also those who advocated social equality between the races. These persons were warned to leave the neighborhood, and if they did not leave they suffered serious consequences. Usually one warning was enough, and the person who had incurred the displeasure of the Klan was only too glad to flee.

The Klansmen always organized on a military or a semi-military basis, and included in their organization many of the men who had served in the cavalry of the Confederate Army. They had proved themselves formidable foes on many battlefields. All were expert riders and good shots. Their weapons were usually the old style cap and ball Colt six-shooter, which was such an effective weapon in the hands of the Confederate and Union cavalry.

On rare occasions the Ku Kluxers would invade the quarters of an obnoxious carpetbag county judge or prosecuting attorney and shoot him offhand, two or three members of the "Den" acting as executioners.

Any public official who used his office to oppress a citizen in any way was speedily made aware of the fact that the Klan had its eye on him. The local "Dens," while themselves operating in defiance of all law, exercised a salutary effect in preserving law and order during reconstruction.

Encounters often reaching the magnitude of small pitched battles occasionally occurred between the negro militia and the Klansmen. When this happened victory nearly always perched upon the standard of the "Flaming Cross."

The Klan, too, made its force felt in another way, which was almost as effective as its violent methods. The carpetbaggers, negro officers, and other persons who had incurred the dislike of the Southern population, were rigidly ostracized. They were ignored in all the walks of life, and in churches, schools and public meetings, as well as in all business matters; an effective personal boycott was established against them. With this in operation it was not very long before many of the carpetbag officers thought the county too unpleasant or unhealthy for them, and they migrated back to the North from whence they had come. The consequence of this policy was that many of the invaders from the North were also forced to associate only with the negroes, and few of them could stand treatment of that kind long. The policy of ostracizing obnoxious officials and others proved as effective in causing them to seek new pastures as the more violent operations of the Klansmen.

Because the membership and operations of the Klan were invariably held in secret, it was often put in a position where it could not defend itself against accusations which were made against it. Many crimes and misdemeanors were perpetrated in the South in these times by other than Klansmen, who used the Order to cover their personal misdeeds. Then, too, as in every organization, bad men gained admission to the "Dens," and some of them used their membership in the Order to satisfy private hatreds and grudges on their neighbors.

CHAPTER VII

A REAL INVISIBLE EMPIRE

We have seen in the new Ku Klux Klan a parallel to
these conditions, in that various disorders occurred, some
years ago, particularly in Louisiana and Texas, that were
traced by the Atlanta Klan Headquarters to men who had
no official connection with the Klan. Wherever this happened the Imperial Wizard, according to evidence obtained at Atlanta headquarters, invariably endeavored to.
assist the local officers in prosecuting the guilty. In all
great organizations undesirable members often secure ad-
mittance, even in the churches and fraternal orders. This
fact is well known to everybody who belongs to a fraternal
order or a church. The Klan in the old days, as well as
in present times, has often been blamed for crimes and
misdemeanors with which it had no connection whatever.

"The Invisible Empire" was well named, for it was
really an invisible empire. While its work was crude and
often violent, it exercised a potent influence in recovering
white supremacy in the South, and was undoubtedly the
chief factor in the political reconstruction of the South
which resulted in the white people regaining control of
their governments. The state and county governments
were in the hands of war governors and other officials,
appointed from Washington, as well as agents of the

50

Freedmen's Bureau, and the military commanders; all were hostile to the Klan.

Repeatedly, in nearly every section where a "Den" existed, the carpetbag authorities made desperate efforts to obtain a list of the members of the Klan and to break up the local "Den." For a former Confederate soldier to be found with a Klan uniform on his premises was always followed by immediate arrest and imprisonment, and in some cases the discovery of the white regalia resulted in a summary execution.

But the Klan was so thoroughly organized everywhere and so bound together by mutual interests that it was rare indeed in Reconstruction times where a military commander was able to discover any of the secrets of the Klan or cause disbandment of a "Den."

Klansmen practiced absolute loyalty to their "Grand Cyclops," and "Den" members maintained the secrecy and the cardinal principles upon which the order was founded. Usually the "Grand Cyclops" was the most prominent citizen in his community and a man of standing, influence, and good character. His assistants were nearly always of the same type, and these level-headed men were dominated only with the purpose to prevent misgovernment and to punish the guilty in their neighborhood. This was the general policy throughout all their local "Dens."

A local 'Den" never had a regular meeting place. This was for the purpose of securing greater secrecy. The local Klan nearly always met at night, when there was moonlight, and usually in woodland or abandoned farming land, where it was unlikely anyone would discover the masked riders at an assembly. Every member of the Klan was obligated to hasten to the meeting place when summoned. The policy that was always followed in regard to persons who had to be corrected in the neighborhood was to consider their case at the Klan's meeting, and it was the invariable practice to first serve warning on the obnoxious one. If he did not speedily reform, another meeting of the Klan decided on his correction. Notices were prepared in an illiterate manner so as to mystify the recipient and better preserve the secrecy. Such warnings were always posted at night. From a study of reconstruction it is evident that the Klan's secret methods certainly subdued or intimidated the negro and bad white men, and caused the white people to feel that an invisible power existed for their protection, under which they felt secure, much more so than they regarded the local laws and the carpetbag officers as means of protection to life and property.

Occasionally it happened that the "Grand Cyclops" of a Klan was an incapable person, and under his leadership the Klan sometimes committed indiscretions in direct contradiction to its principles. Sometimes it occurred that former Confederate soldiers, young men of an adventurous disposition, made up part of the membership of a Klan, and an organization of that kind sometimes deviated from the purpose for which it was organized. Law-abiding and honest men who found themselves in such "Dens" took the first opportunity to withdraw. Many men in these circumstances were glad to renounce their membership without appearing to be traitors to the oath they had taken.

The Klan also played an important part in politics, and in neighborhoods where a "Den" was strongly organized and numerous in membership the members intimidated the negroes and kept them from the polls in elections. Often men in large numbers, who were thought to be Klansmen, attended the polls, and, heavily armed, by a threatening attitude prevented the negroes from electing their candidate. They were thus able to convince the negro that it was not wise for the black race to participate actively in political affairs, and this contributed probably more than any other maneuver of the whites in wresting control of their governments from the hands of the carpet-baggers.

It not infrequently happened that the activity of the local "Den" met the approval of the Federal garrisons, and instances are known of former Union soldiers and officers who settled in the South after the end of the war who were members of the Ku Klux Klan, and who were thoroughly in sympathy with the efforts of the white population to establish law and get control of their government. There was hardly ever personal animosity between Union soldiers who settled in the South after the war and the Confederates. Rather a spirit of soldierly comradeship existed between the former foes. Few indeed of the carpetbag officials or agents of the Freedmen's Bureau had served in the Union Army.

A strategic policy of the Klan, which proved very effective in **preventing** Federal army commanders from tracing their movements or gaining information concerning their night riding, was that non-resident "Dens" would carry on operations, the local "Dens" where the action was taken remaining quiescent. A "Den" near the Alabama State line would raid into Mississippi, riding at night perhaps a distance of 25 or 30 miles, visit punishment on a victim marked out by the Mississippi "Den," and by daylight be back over the Alabama line and disbanded at their homes. Under such procedure it was practically impossible for Federal army commanders to gain any information of the activities of the horsemen who rode by night.

Following is an official order of the Pulaski "Den," published in 1869. Its a type of similar orders and Klan proclamation used throughout the South:

> "Headquarters Realm No. 1,
> Dreadful Era, Black Epoch,
> Dreadful Hour.

"General Order No. 1,

"Whereas, information of an authentic character has reached these headquarters that the blacks in the counties of Marshall, Maury, Giles, and Lawrence are organized into military companies, with the avowed purpose to make war upon and exterminate the Ku Klux Klan, said blacks are hereby solemnly warned and ordered to desist from further action in such organizations, if they exist.

"The Grand Dragon regrets the necessity of such an order. But this Klan shall not be outraged and interfered with by lawless negroes and meaner white men, who do not and never have understood our purpose.

"In the first place this Klan is not an institution of violence, lawlessness, and cruelty; it is not lawless; it is not aggressive; it is not military; it is not revolutionary.

"It is, essentially, originally, and inherently a protective organization. It proposes to execute law instead of resisting it; and to protect all good men, whether white or black, from the outrages and atrocities of bad men of both colors, who have been for the past three years a terror to society and an injury to us all.

"The blacks seem to be impressed with the belief that this Klan is especially their enemy. We are not the enemy of the blacks, as long as they behave themselves, make no threats upon us, and do not attack or interfere with us.

"But if they make war upon us they must abide the awful retribution that will follow.

"This Klan while in its peaceful movements, and disturbing no one, has been fired into three times. This will not be endured any longer; and if it occurs again, and the parties be discovered, a remorseless vengeance will be wreaked upon them.

"We reiterate that we are for peace and law and order. No man, white or black, shall be molested for his political sentiments.

"Outrages have been perpetrated by irresponsible parties in the name of this Klan. Should such parties be apprehended, they will be dealt with in a manner to insure us future exemption from such imposition. These imposters have, in some instances, whipped negroes. This is wrong! It is denounced by this Klan, as it must be by all good and humane men."

CHAPTER VIII

VIII. DISBANDMENT OF THE KLAN

The activities of the Ku Klux Klan aroused great hostility among the war governors, carpetbag officials, agents of the Freedmen's Bureau, and the Federal military commanders.

The first legislative action by a Southern State to curb the activity of the Klan was begun in 1868. In September of that year Governor Brownlow, familiarly known as "Parson" Brownlow, war and reconstruction governor of Tennessee, called the State Legislature in session and had an act passed placing a rigid ban on the Klan. This act provided that any person who had any connection with the Klan was to be fined not less than $500 and imprisoned in the penitentiary for not less than five years. To give aid or comfort, or to shelter or feed any Ku Kluxer subjected any person to the same penalty. In an endeavor to make the statute effective, informers were to receive, where a conviction occurred, half of the $500 fine. This law also provided that any citizen had authority to summarily arrest a Klansman anywhere within the bounds of the state without process of law, and it even went so far as to give authority to any citizen to arrest a person under suspicion of being a Klansman. Few arrests were made, and the law was practically a dead letter. The Klan was particularly well organized at that time in Tennessee, having about 40,000 members. Instead of informers prosecuting the Klansmen, the new law at first had the effect of increasing the determination of the white population to assist the Klan more than ever. "Parson" Brownlow made vigorous efforts to enforce the law while he was governor of Tennessee, but was not able to accomplish much toward breaking up the Klan in that state.

Notwithstanding the severe provisions of the law, the Klan operated in Tennessee successfully for nearly a year afterwards. It disbanded, not because of the law, but because conditions had changed. The Tennessee law was followed by similar action in other states, notably Alabama and Mississippi. Alabama passed a law in 1868 modeled on the Tennessee law, and the Mississippi Legislature acted in 1870. Two years later the Congressional investigation of the Klan occurred. All these laws were passed by carpetbag legislators and governors.

In February, 1869, Gen. Nathan Bedford Forrest, the "Grand Wizard" of the organization, issued a proclamation to the members of the "Invisible Empire." This proclamation described the action of the Tennessee Legislature against the Klan, and went on to state that the Klan had largely accomplished the purpose for which it had been organized, and that robbery, crime, and lawlessness had been suppressed. Present conditions, said the "Grand Wizard," afforded adequate protection to property, life, and society." The South was not longer fearful for lives or property. The "Grand Wizard" declared that he had complete authority to do anything that he wished for the benefit of the Order, and he therefore declared the Klan dissolved and disbanded. The proclamation was addressed to all of the subdivisions of the "Invisible Empire." Some of the Klans obeyed the proclamation and some did not. In Tennessee the "Dens" were soon disbanded because that state had recovered Constitutional government and the reconstruction regime had practically ended.

Though many "Dens" were disbanded in Tennessee in 1869 and 1870, in other states, particularly Mississippi and Alabama, the local Klans continued their operations as late as the fall of 1873.

Nathan Bedford Forrest was undoubtedly the best man in the entire South to serve the organization as the "Grand Wizard." He acquired a reputation as a great cavalry strategian, tactician, and hard fighter in the Confederate Army during the Civil War, second to no other general in either Union or Confederate army. A man of dauntless courage, great resourcefulness, and unbounded energy, he was an ideal "Grand Wizard" of the "Invisible Empire." pire."

By the end of 1873 the local "Dens" as constituted subdivisions of the "Invisible Empire," were practically disbanded throughout the entire South. They ceased their work as organized Klansmen, but the same movement with many of the same men continued at intervals for several years afterwards. This was done despite the fact that after 1873 conditions in the South had greatly changed, the white inhabitants had been able to reestablish Constitutional government nearly everywhere, and to take control of their political affairs.

Though the Klansmen as Klansmen were disbanded, other organizations continued under the names of "The White League," the "White Brotherhood," "Pale Faces," "Constitutional Union Guards," and "Knights of the White Camelia." The "Knights of the White Camelia" were strong, particularly in Louisiana, practically the entire Klan membership arraying themselves in the ranks of the new Knights.

In examining old records and documents of the original Ku Klux Klan interesting rituals were discovered. For instance, the initiation oath of the "White Brotherhood" was as follows:

"You solemnly swear in the presence of the Almighty God, that you will never reveal the name of the person who initiated you; and that you will never reveal what is now about to come to your knowledge; and that you are not now a member of the Red String Order, Union League, Heroes of America, Grand Army of the Republic, or any other organization whose aim and intention is to destroy the rights of the South, or of the States, or of the people, or to elevate the negro to political equality with themselves; and that you are opposed to all such principles; so help you God."

All these organizations gradually went out of existence and by 1880 it is probable there were no Ku Klux "Dens" or units of the other organizations in existence.

The real reason for the gradual disappearance of the Ku Klux Klan and its successors under various names was that the unbearable political conditions existing in the

Southern States from 1865 to 1873 had disappeared. The Klan and its successors vanished with these conditions.

Undoubtedly the flight of the carpetbaggers, withdrawal of the Freedmen's Bureau agents and military commanders, and the substitution of Constitutional state government for military rule were the real factors which abolished the Ku Klux Klan and its successors. Had reconstruction conditions in the South continued the Klan would have existed coincident with these conditions.

Daniel H. Chamberlain, Reconstruction governor of South Carolina, said concerning the Southern white man of his day:

"I consider him a distinct and really noble growth of our American soil. For if fortitude under good and under evil fortune, if endurance without complaint of what comes in the tide of human affairs, if a grim clinging to ideals once charming, if vigor and resiliency of character and spirit under defeat and poverty and distress, if a steady love of learning and letters when libraries were lost in flames and the wreckage of war, if self-restraint when the long-delayed relief at last came—if, I say, all these qualities are parts of real heroism, if these qualities can vivify and ennoble a man or a people, then our own South may lay claim to an honored place among the differing types of our great common race."

The Ku Klux Klan had accomplished the purpose for which it was organized. However much opinion in the North may differ as to the justification for the organization it is probable that almost the entire native white population of the South backed the Klan, and all Southern men were either active members of the "Dens," or secret sympathizers.

Methods of reconstruction of the South by the victorious North are now recognized to have been too drastic and in many instances indefensible. Such a policy brought together every element in the South against the Republican Party, and we have inherited from those days the "Solid South," which exists today, and which seventy-five years after the Civil War still presents in the Democratic Party an unbreakable front of political opposition to the Republican Party. The Ku Klux Klan was only a manifestation of the spirit of opposition to reconstruction measures taken by the North, and the masked rider in his white robe was a symbol of the spirit of the South in revolt against carpetbag government and negro misrule. These are facts that cannot be explained away, and today our Northern historians, no matter how unpalatable the facts, recognize that conditions existing in the South in reconstruction times were intolerable.

Time is a great healer of all hatreds and all feuds, and the passing years have done much to nullify the spirit of resentment which stirred the South in reconstruction days, but that section has inherited and still possesses the "Solid South" as a tangible result of reconstruction as administered by the North. The Republican Party, except in rare instances where political landslides have occurred in presidential elections, has never since the Civil War been able to establish itself firmly in the South despite repeated efforts. This is largely the result of the reconstruction policy of the North after the Civil War, and in many sections of the South today the Republican Party is still regarded with a bitter hatred which is hardly understandable by a new generation in the North.

As the South had been defeated on the battlefields and was absolutely bankrupt after Appomattox, the Southern people were not in a position to start another armed rebellion. But the organization of the Ku Klux Klan undoubtedly was a form of rebellion against the tyranny of reconstruction policies.

The American Colonies revolted from Great Britain in 1776, under provocations that were not nearly as irksome and irritating as the conditions which were imposed on the South during reconstruction.

The Ku Klux Klan, therefore, indirectly is partly responsible today for the political situation in the United States. This organization exerted a profound influence on our national history.

All of the smaller organizations which succeeded the Ku Klux Klan, while not as effective or as well organized as the parent body, were in some states equally as active.

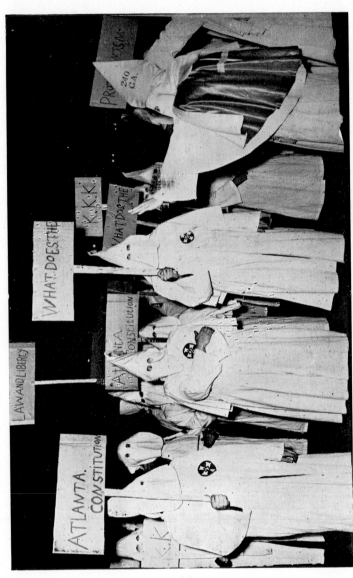

Klansmen picketing the *Atlanta Constitution*, Georgia daily newspaper opposed to the Klan.

CHAPTER IX

THE FIRST CONGRESSIONAL
INVESTIGATION

State, county, and city elections in the South in 1870, when the white population was engaged in taking control of government from the carpetbaggers, and control of State Legislatures was seized by the whites, who ousted negro state senators and representatives, caused much turmoil and excitement south of the Mason and Dixon line. The Ku Klux Klan participated largely in these elections and was a potent factor in overthrowing carpetbag and negro rule. There were many affrays at the polls, and the Ku Kluxers, as well as other Southern men, used the six-shooter and the shotgun as a method of direct persuasion at many election places. The negroes were intimidated and prevented from voting in hundreds of places, and the carpetbagger, if he insisted upon participating in elections, was terrified by open threats of violence, which often culminated in shooting affrays. In this year the whites really regained control of their own political affairs in the South.

Professor Walter Henry Cook, of the Western Reserve University, of Cleveland, Ohio, a Northerner, in his "Secret Political Societies in the South During the Period of Reconstruction," says:

"The Ku Klux accomplished much. From a political viewpoint it secured home rule for several of the Southern States. It ended the disgraceful rule of the carpetbaggers therein, and it helped to reestablish honest and efficient governmental institutions. This example was an inspiration which, after 1872, soon led the men of the Southern States, still in radical control, to the glorious victory in regaining self-government.

"From an economical standpoint, the negroes were frightened into going to work and were prevented to a large extent from breaking labor contracts. These were important services in the rehabilitation of the South.

"From a social standpoint, the Klan protected property, protected life, and brought order out of chaos."

Woodrow Wilson, War President of the United States, in his "History of the American People," says:

"Adventurers swarmed out of the North, as much the enemies of one race as of the other, to cozen, beguile and use the negroes. The white men were aroused by a mere instinct of self-preservation until at last there sprang into existence a great Ku Klux Klan, a veritable Empire of the South, to protect the Southern Country."

Many accounts of the election disorders were published in the Northern newspapers, and much excitement and resentment over the situation existed in the North. Northern newspapers of that period bitterly denounced the Southern people and their election methods. Finally Congress, responsive to the agitation and anti-Klan propaganda in the North, which was directed more at the Ku

Klux Klan than at the Southern People as a people, on April 20, 1871, passed the Ku Klux Act. Briefly described, this law authorized the President to suspend the writ of habeas corpus in order to effectively deal with the Ku Klux Klan and the other brotherhoods, which were termed "conspiracies," and it enlarged the powers of the Federal courts. A congressional committee was appointed to investigate "All affairs in the late insurrectionary states." Subcommittees of this committee held hearings in Washington and visited the South, accumulated a great amount of evidence which fills 13 volumes, copies of which repose on dust-covered shelves in the Congressional Library. The investigation had two important results. From it the Ku Klux Klan was brought to realize the danger of their Order and similar organizations by interference of Congressional committees instigated in the North. The investigation convinced Ku Klux members who had determined upon continuing the Klan organization that it would be best to dissolve the Klan, and those Southern white men who had advocated disbanding the Klans were encouraged by the Congressional committee. The result was that the remaining Klan organizations in nearly every section were dissolved.

The Ku Klux Klan had officially ceased to exist, previous to the Congressional investigation, however, by proclamation of the "Grand Wizard," General Forrest The imperial edict was issued in March, 1869, when the Klan was dissolved.

Prior to the passage of the Ku Klux Act, Congress, spurred on by the activities of the Ku Klux Klan, and encouraged by the clamour in the North against the Klan, passed on May 31, 1870, the "Enforcement Act." This was planned to protect the rights of citizens to vote in all elections" without distinction of color or race." The act conferred upon United States courts the authority to punish persons going in disguise upon highways, or who operated disguised for the purpose of intimidating or preventing a citizen exercising his electoral rights. The old "Civil Rights Act" of 1866 was incorporated in the new enforcement act, and the principal provision of the 1866 law was to be enforced by the Federal Courts. In 1871 Congress passed a supplementary Enforcement Act which strengthened the Enforcement Act of May 31, 1870. President Grant called the attention of Congress to the disorderly condition at elections in the South, and the Ku Klux Act was then passed. The crux of the Ku Klux Act was that where alleged "unlawful conspiracies," such as the Ku Klux Klan was considered to be by the Republican majority in Congress and the Grant Administration, existed, the writ of habeas corpus could be suspended by the President and he could use the military and naval forces of the United States to enforce the act. The Ku Klux Act was in fact a bestowal upon the chief magistrate of arbitrary power of the army and navy to put down disorders in the South. It was, of course, aimed principally at the Ku Klux Klan. The enforcement of this legislation, where Federal troops were employed at the polls in the South, almost caused another armed insurrection and led to continued agitation and acts of violence between Southern men and Federal soldiers.

Enforcement of the Ku Klux Act and the Enforcement Act caused more disorders than before, and the legislation did not result in the suppression of the Ku Klux and similar orders because the Ku Klux as an organization had already ceased to exist in 1869 by the edict of the "Grand Wizard." The law in some sections brought a veritable reign of terror. Prominent citizens who were under suspicion of being Ku Kluxers or sympathizers of the organization were often seized arbitrarily by orders of military commanders and thrown into jail, where they remained without trial, and where they were kept at the whim of the Federal authorities.

In 1883 the United States Supreme Court declared unconstitutional interference by Congress with elections in the South. The damage, however, had already been done, and the effect of the law, which the Southern people believed oppressed them politically and socially, only had the effect of rendering more stubborn the resistance to Federal authority and the soldiers by the Southern white man. It further consolidated and strengthened the "Solid South" as a political entity.

Impartial historians are now agreed that it was a mistake on the part of Congress to attempt to coerce the South, and it was also impolitic for any power to attempt to cause the Anglo-Saxon race in the South to become submerged under a black political wave. The real roots of the Ku Klux Klan can be traced back to those qualities of the Anglo-Saxon race, existing both in the North and the South, which forbade amalgamation of the white blood with an inferior race, and the possession of a spirit which was determined to be dominant in government at all hazards. Had conditions been reversed the Northern people undoubtedly would have acted exactly as did the Southerners.

In 1872 Congress passed an act restoring the right to vote and to hold office by the former Confederates, and it was not long before the able white leaders in the South had taken direction of all political affairs in that part of the country. The disorderly conditions gradually disappeared, Federal troops were withdrawn, and the South really began her political recovery. The era of war reconstruction ended.

Sentiment in Congress and the North against the Ku Klux Klan and the terrible political and social conditions which prevailed in the South prior to 1870 was not all one way, and opinion as to these conditions and concerning the Ku Klux Klan was divided in the North. This is shown by the fact that the Congressional Committee which investigated the Ku Klux Klan presented majority and minority reports. The majority reports set forth that a "Southern conspiracy" of a political nature existed against constitutional law and the negro race. The minority report stated that misgovernment and exploitation of the South by reconstruction officials had provoked the natural resentment and resistance of the people of that section.

Thus the carpetbaggers and the negro legislatures were officially condemned by a congressional committee, though in a minority report.

Before the passage of the Ku Klux Act there had been many stirring debates in Congress concerning Southern conditions. These, carried by the press, served to inform Northern people as to the real conditions in the South.

After 1872 agitation concerning the Ku Klux practically ended. A better feeling began to prevail in the South. The North, too, realized the disadvantages under which the Southern people had labored, and the two sections once divided by a fratricidal strife began to have a more friendly feeling.

The Spanish-American War, in 1898, recemented both sections and performed the final act of reunion which again welded the Republic into a coherent whole. The son or grandson of the man who wore the Confederate gray, who marched and fought and died by the side of his "bunkie," a grandson or a son of the man who had worn the Union blue, both fighting to free the Cuban, both fighting to strike off the shackles of Spanish tyranny from a helpless people and an oppressed but alien race, did more to unite the North and the South than all the reconstruction laws passed by Congress and all the agitation since 1865.

In Washington, D. C., there was a Camp of the United Spanish-American War Veterans in which one of the most honored and active members was a Confederate veteran.

The World War further brought the men of the North and the South and their descendants together, and today the United States knows no North and no South, no East and no West. We are all one glorious American family, if we can ever Americanize our big alien population, and expel from our shores the Communists, the Nazis, the Fascists, and all the other un-American aliens.

CHAPTER X

ORIGIN OF THE NEW KLAN

Every great national movement always has behind it a man with an idea. The man behind the modern Ku Klux Klan when first organized was Col. William Joseph Simmons,[1] of Atlanta, Georgia, first "Imperial Wizard" of the new Klan. The primary idea which animated the founder of the new Klan was patriotism, Americanism, and the supremacy of the Caucasion race.

Colonel Simmons is a remarkable man, mentally and physically. He admirably filled the part of "Imperial Wizard," to which office he had been elected for life by the Knights of the "Invisible Empire."[2] In most spheres of life Colonel Simmons would have been a great success. Impressions of the ruler of the Invisible Empire were gained by the writer from many personal interviews with Colonel Simmons and close association with him for some time in Atlanta, the headquarters of the Klan, and during the second Congressional investigation in Washington.

---

[1] Col. Simmons got his military title as colonel of a regiment of uniformed Woodmen of the World. He was a private in the War with Spain, in an Alabama Volunteer regiment. He is now living in retirement at Luverne, Ala.
[2] Now has no connection with the Klan.

He is a remarkable man in many ways. He is 6 feet 2 inches tall, weighs about 220 pounds, is perfectly proportioned, has a most engaging personality, and the whole impression of the man is pleasing. His manner is always cordial and gracious to a stranger, and his assistants and those who knew him personally in Atlanta respect and love him. Colonel Simmons has a well-developed sense of humor and likes to tell anecdotes and crack jokes with his friends. In other ages this man undoubtedly would have risen high, for he has an imposing and majestic presence and great ability. Common sense, calm judgment, and a vast experience dominate his every action. There was at all times surrounding him an air of dignity, and he was at the same time affable to all. His disposition is kindly, and he possesses a courageous and charitable heart. Colonel Simmons is a fearless man, and he has never paid attention to the innumerable anonymous communications threatening his life, which the Klan used to continually receive in Atlanta. He went about Atlanta unattended and unarmed the same as any citizen bent upon his daily business.

Before and after the Congressional investigation, however, his host of friends insisted that some precautions be taken to prevent his assassination, which was threatened by numerous signed and unsigned letters. So against his protests guards were provided for his home, and for the Imperial Palace, then headquarters for the Klan in Atlanta. These guards were mostly volunteers and members of the Atlanta Klan. They served in relays night and day for a long time.

Colonel Simmons sprang from that sturdy Scotch-Irish and English stock that carved out a new government and a new land in the South and the West.

An investigation of the personal history of the man convinced the observer of two things concerning this really remarkable personage:

1. The many experiences of his life illustrate his untiring energy, indomitable courage, and complete devotion to any work, cause, or ideal in which he may be engaged.

2. All of his past experiences had been merely a training for his work in establishing the Knights of the Ku Klux Klan.

Colonel Simmons has been in turn a student, soldier, Methodist minister, and an organizer for fraternal orders. In all of these occupations he was a conspicuous success.

Born on a farm in Alabama, his boyhood was spent in agricultural pursuits. His father was a practicing physician, and the boy desired to follow in his parent's footsteps. The Simmons family was not rich, and the income derived from the father's country practice and from the farm was not sufficient to give the youth the medical education he had determined to secure. He went to a wealthy uncle and asked him to advance the money to pay for a medical education. His uncle informed him, if he would work his way through the first year of a medical college, he, the uncle, would loan him the money necessary to pay for the remaining years of the course.

Young Simmons for two years took a preliminary medical course under a special preceptor of Johns Hopkins University, of Baltimore, Maryland, paying his expenses by work of various kinds outside of study hours. He finished his first two years with credit. When he saw his uncle and told him what he had done, and asked this relative to advance the money for the remainder of his medical course his uncle informed the young student that he was only joking when he promised to loan the money. This crushed Simmons completely for the time being and temporarily destroyed his optimistic and youthful faith in human nature, he said. He could not understand why his own uncle would repudiate a solemn promise. Unable to secure the money to finish his medical education, the aspiring young man did not know what to do.

The war with Spain began, and he determined to adopt a military career. He went to the nearest recruiting station, enlisted in the 1st Alabama Volunteer Infantry, plunging into military life with the same earnestness of purpose which characterized him in all other studies. He had been in camp but a few days when he asked one of his officers where he could secure a book on military tactics, for he had already determined to quickly master military tactics and devote his life to the Army. Colonel Simmons remembers to this day the reply of the officer when he asked him where he could secure a book on tactics.

The officer said: "What in hell do you want with a book on military tactics?"

The raw recruit insisted that he must get a book on tactics, and he gave the officer all the money he had to buy the book for him. When he secured the textbook he studied it at night when the regiment was sleeping. The result was that he advanced more rapidly in military knowledge than the other men of his company, and at the end of the war was preparing to remain in the Army. As soon as he was honorably discharged, his discharge reading: "Services honest and faithful," he hastened back to his Alabama home and there took up again the burden of helping support his mother and the other children.

The young veteran, back on the farm, was converted at a Methodist camp meeting—"got the old-time religion," as he expresses it. The conversion was thorough, for young Simmons determined to become a minister.

While Colonel Simmons is a man of intense action in many lines of endeavor, he is also a dreamer. All great men in history have been men of action and men of dreams. The "Imperial Wizard" says he does not believe in visions, and yet he relates a mysterious and interesting occurrence which he says he does not understand to this day. He was then a poor minister in Alabama, and one summer night was sitting at his window watching the clouds as they drifted in front of the moon. Suddenly he thought he caught sight of something mysterious and strange in the sky, and as he looked at the clouds a row of horses seemed to be galloping across the horizon. White-robed figures were on the steeds. The clouds seemed to disperse, and a rough outline of the United States appeared as a background. The horses remained, and then one big problem after another of American life moved across the map.

He fell to his knees and offered a prayer to God, so

he said, to help solve the mystery of the apparitions he had seen in the sky. He then registered a vow that a great patriotic fraternal order should be builded as a memorial to the heroes of our nation.

That was the real beginning of the Knights of the Ku Klux Klan, he says, and set him to dreaming of the time when he would be able to create the present organization of the "Invisible Empire," now existing throughout the United States.

Readers will smile or scoff at this story, but it is a well-known fact that men who have headed great movements have seen visions, or thought they saw them. Scientists have explained this phenomenon as a psychic manifestation of unconscious desires, but to the dreamer it seems a visible materialization of what is probably a figment of an excited imagination.

In the ministry Colonel Simmons manifested the same admirable qualities that he had shown all his life. Many circuits where he served the preacher had never received more than $250 salary a year, and the charge had paid nothing toward the appropriation for various church causes. All the circuits that he served immediately took on new life and showed a remarkable growth. Untrained in the arts of elocution when he began to preach, Minister Simmons rapidly developed into one of the most powerful and eloquent orators in the South. His ability as a speaker was acquired by experience only, yet he became one of the most polished orators in American life, able to hold great meetings spellbound by his eloquence. He was equally at home in pulpit or on platform.

COL. WILLIAM JOSEPH SIMMONS
Second Imperial Wizard and Founder of the New Klan. Not now connected with the Klan.

CHAPTER XI

COLONEL SIMMONS A FRATERNAL
ORGANIZER

Minister Simmons needed money for his family and dependent relations, and he then entered into the fraternal and insurance field. In this work his ability and force soon carried him to the front, and in a short time he was given charge of an entire district in South Georgia for one of the largest fraternal orders.[1] Soon he had built up a fraternal insurance business which gave him an income of $10,000 a year. He was commissioned as a "Colonel" by the Woodmen of the World to command and organize regiments of their uniform rank. That is where he got his title. At that time he was the youngest man in the order holding such rank.

Soon after he moved to Atlanta, and was standing, one day, on a street corner talking to friends when a large touring automobile skidded around a corner. The back bumper struck him in the spine, and he fell to the pavement completely paralyzed. He was bedridden for six months, and during this time, when he had nothing to do but think, he conceived and worked out the details of the plan of the Knights of the Ku Klux Klan; to build the order about which he had dreamed for years. He had been quietly working and thinking out a plan to do this

---

[1] Woodmen of the World.

for fifteen years, ever since his "vision in the sky," but it was not until he was laid up in bed, seriously injured, that he came to a resolution to launch the big enterprise as soon as he recovered.

The accident ended his career as an influential and powerful factor in the fraternal insurance business, and had it not been for the accident it is probable he would still be one of the chief officers of that fraternity.

In discussing his life with his friends, and when in a reminiscent mood, Colonel Simmons expresses his belief that it may be possible that a higher power took him from the four distinct phases of activity into which he had previously entered, and finally forced him into his work as head of the Knights of the Ku Klux Klan, which he considers the greatest movement ever started for the preservation, elevation, and strengthening of the Caucasian race. He was prevented when he had determined to become a great doctor, he was not able to devote his life to the military service of his country, he left a ministerial career of great promise, and when he had achieved large success in his work in the fraternal insurance business he was kept from that career by an accident.

All these experiences in life made Colonel Simmons a wise and thoughtful man. His habit of mind is extremely calm and deliberate, and hatred and passion never disturb his thoughts. He is a real Christian, and his heart is always responsive to the calls of unfortunate humanity. His experience as a medical student was valuable, his service in the Army during the Spanish-American War taught him discipline, his career in the Methodist Church broadened his mind and made him a great orator, and his work as an organizer of fraternal societies taught him business methods and gave him an insight into the customs of men everywhere. Thus, when he began his organization of the Knights of the Ku Klux Klan, he was as well qualified for this work as any man in the United States.

Colonel Simmons has been married for many years to an estimable woman who came from a prominent Southern family. His wife is an invalid. He had one son.

Colonel Simmons for more than fifteen years had been revolving in his mind the organization of the Ku Klux Klan. He intended to continue not only the visible, physical organization of the Ku Klux Klan, as a memorial, but principally to perpetuate its spiritual purpose, and to make it a national, standard, fraternal order composed of American manhood, who believe in preservation of pure Anglo-Saxon institutions, ideals, and principles. There was also the thought to keep alive the memory of the original Klan, and to collect historical accounts of its work, principles, and institutions. The new invisible empire of the Ku Klux Klan was to be, also, a lasting and living memorial to the old Klansmen. Anybody who knows Colonel Simmons and the high officers of the Knights of the Ku Klux Klan who were carrying on the work must be convinced that the announced plans of the new Knights of the Ku Klux Klan were founded upon right principles, and that it was to be a great and patriotic American organization.

Colonel Simmons has always taken great interest in fraternal orders and he is a member in good standing in fifteen such organizations, including the Blue Lodge Masons and Knights Templars.

There was no thought in the mind of Colonel Simmons, he said, to revive in any way the night-riding, masked operations of the original Ku Klux Klan, for conditions in the South do not justify such an organization today, but the principal thought around which centered the idea of reestablishing the Ku Klux Klan was its lofty spiritual purpose, he said, to be manifested in the new organization which would constitute a great American patriotic and fraternal order.

In October, 1915, Simmons called together a few friends in Atlanta, Georgia. Among them were three members of the original Klan. Every person with whom Colonel Simmons conferred was enthusiastic for reviving the old Klan, or organizing a new one, and in the same month thirty-four citizens of Atlanta, many of them the most prominent in Georgia, held a meeting and signed a petition for a charter of the New Knights of the Ku Klux Klan.

As the Klan had among its thirty-four charter members three of the horsemen of the famous old Ku Klux it was declared to be the only legitimate heir of the parent organization of reconstruction days, and therefore possessed the sole rights to all of its regalia, ritual, and symbols. Each year since 1915 the Klan has held an anniversary celebration, on May 6, the date on which the old Klan was officially founded. This annual celebration takes the form of public parades throughout the South with the Klansmen dressed in the official white costumes.

With the original thirty-four members, and from this small beginning, the Klan has spread until it has branches in nearly every State in the Union, and its membership runs into many thousands.

The following proclamation was issued by Colonel Simmons after the Klan was organized:

"To all Nations, Peoples, Tribes and Tongues, and to the Lovers of Law and Order, Peace and Justice, of the Whole Earth, Greetings:

"I, and the citizens of the Invisible Empire through me, proclaim to you as follows:

"We, the members of this Order, desiring to promote real patriotism toward our civil government; honorable peace among men and nations; protection for and happiness in the homes of our people; love, real brotherhood, mirth and manhood among ourselves, justice and fraternity among all mankind; and believing we can best accomplish these noble purposes through the channel of a high-class mystic, social, patriotic, benevolent association, having a perfected lodge system, with an exalted ritualistic form of work and an effective form of government, not for selfish profit but for the mutual betterment, benefit and protection of all our oathbound associates, their welfare physically, socially, morally and vocationally, and their loved ones, do proclaim to the whole world that we are dedicated to the sublime and pleasant duty of providing generous aid, tender sympathy and fraternal assistance in the effulgence of the light of life and amid the sable shadows of death; amid fortune and misfortune, and the exalted privilege of demonstrating the practical utility of the great, yet most neglected, doctrine of the Fatherhood of God and Brotherhood of Man as a vital force in the lives and affairs of men.

"In this we invite all men who can qualify to become citizens of the Invisible Empire, to approach the portal of our beneficent domain and join us in our noble work of extending its boundaries; in disseminating the gospel of KLANKRAFT, thereby encouraging, conserving, protecting and making vital the fraternal human relationship in the practice of a wholesome clannishness; to share with us the glory of performing the sacred duty of protecting womanhood; to maintain forever white supremacy in all things; to commemorate the holy and chivalric achievements of our fathers; to safeguard the sacred rights, exalted privileges and distinctive institutions of our civil government; to bless mankind, and to keep eternally ablaze the sacred fire of a fervent devotion to a pure Americanism.

"The Invisible Empire is founded on sterling character, and immutable principles, based upon a most sacred sentiment and cemented by noble purposes; it is promoted by a sincere, unselfish devotion of the souls of many men and is managed and governed by the consecrated intelligence of thoughtful brains. It is the soul of chivalry and virtue's impenetrable shield, the devout impulse of an unconquered race."

Colonel Simmons was for a time President of the University of America, formerly Lanier University, at Atlanta. This university was bought by the Ku Klux Klan and reorganized. It was not conducted as a Ku Klux Klan university, but as a non-sectarian institution for the youth of the South and the North. The courses were all elective, except Bible study and study of American history and institutions, which was required of all students. A few years ago, however, Lanier University was discontinued. Plans are now being made to reestablish this university and make it one of the largest educational institutions in the country. It probably will have a preparatory school where the poor white boys and girls of the North and South can secure splendid educational privileges free or at cost. Negotiations are under way for additional land in the suburbs of Atlanta, and the Klan plans to make the University of America one of the really great educational institutions in the country. The Klan plans to raise a $5,000,000 endowment fund. The university was named in honor of the famous southern poet, Sidney Lanier. Lanier University existed in Augusta, Georgia, before the War Between the States. During the war it was discontinued, to be revived in Atlanta by Colonel Simmons.

CHAPTER XII

STATEMENT OF COLONEL SIMMONS

Colonel Simmons made the following statement to the author regarding the Invisible Empire and the Knights of the Ku Klux Klan soon after it was organized:

"Throughout the annals of the ages in all recorded movements for the betterment of humanity, whether by revolt against tyranny or along more peaceful lines, we see the manifestation of what justly may be termed the 'Ku Klux Spirit' — the spirit that rebels at oppression and even defies law itself when that law, measured by all the standards of wisdom, justice and moderation, is tyrannical and the instrument of despotism. It is the antithesis of tyranny and the foe of despotism.

"From the time the human race was created, running through all the ages and characteristic of all peoples of all lands, the Ku Klux spirit has fostered freedom and fought tyranny to the death because Ku Kluxism is the very 'antithesis of tyranny' and has never in history been the agency of wrong. It has been the one weapon left to the hand of mankind when mightier forces had shackled him or had taken from him his civil or religious liberty. It has been the ceaseless working of this unquenchable and unconquerable spirit, forced as it has been on innumerable occasions to develop its strength and plan its campaign in secret, that has set the heel of the oppressed on the neck of the oppressor in the battle of Right against Might.

"Before the great Persian Empire was created there was an organization formed for the purpose of enforcing justice. It worked secretly, and it was impelled by the intolerable conditions surrounding conduct of the courts to reverse numerous decisions in which there was open and brazen miscarriage of justice. Its emblem was the star and crescent—symbolic of the sovereignty of justice.

"True, this organization did its work in secret and took the law into its own hands (so to speak), but the attitude and purpose of this early order, which was one of the first recorded manifestations of the 'Ku Klux Spirit,' hundreds of years later was indorsed by no less an authority than Thomas Jefferson when he declared:

" 'Rebellion against tyrants is obedience to God.'

"And by Patrick Henry, when he shouted in defiance of the tyrannical British parliament:

" 'Give me liberty or give me death.'

"The history of Continental Europe is filled with instances in which men who were oppressed and who saw no relief in sight by open rebellion because of the superior power of the oppressor, have banded themselves together in secret with an oathbound determination to die if by death alone they could free themselves from the rule of the tyrant. Man of the Anglo-Saxon stock is a sovereign being and he will wear no man's yoke.

'The followers of Calvin and of Luther and of John Knox in Scotland exemplified to a high degree the Ku

Klux spirit. Because of the fewness of their numbers and because they faced death or imprisonment if they waged their fight in the open, they carried on their work in secret until they felt the time was opportune to bring the issue to a head.

"The spirit that prompted the followers of Calvin, Luther and Knox was identical with the spirit that actuated our Revolutionary fathers and the men of the South in the Reconstruction period.

"The American colonies rebelled against constituted authority and against the iniquitous tax laws imposed upon them by England because the laws were unjust and therefore tyrannical, and because they saw the rights and liberties for which they had braved the unknown terrors of the sea and the unexplored wilds of the New World, rapidly receding to the vanishing point.

"They fully understood the superior power arrayed against them and they realized that the 'little leaven that leaveneth the whole lump' must be started working before they openly challenged the power of British arms. Thus it came to pass that long before the 'shot heard 'round the world' was fired the mighty force was secretly put in operation that cemented the colonies in their determination of 'liberty or death,' and that made possible the greatest monument of all time to liberty and justice—the Republic of the United States of America.

"In Revolutionary history we have two noteworthy manifestations of the Ku Klux spirit. One was the 'Charleston Tea Party' and the other the 'Boston Tea Party,' which occurred four days after the former. In the first instance the outraged citizens of the Colonies recorded their wrath against the tyrannous taxes of the British Government by boarding with arms in their hands, and sank the tea ships by boring holes in their bottoms.

"In the case of the Boston Tea Party the Colonists disguised themselves as Indians, boarded the British tea ships and dumped their cargoes into the sea.

"The only difference between the members of the Boston Tea Party and the members of the Ku Klux Klan of the Reconstruction period following the Civil War was that the former were disguised as Indians while the latter disguised themselves with masks and flowing robes. The actuating cause and the spiritual purpose of the men in both instances was the same.

"Thus we come down to that much misunderstood and shamefully slandered organization of the Reconstruction period which manifested on the largest scale of which we have any record, the Ku Klux spirit, and which made famous the name by which this spirit—the spirit of opposition to tyranny and oppression in any form—has become known.

When the roar of the guns ceased and the smoke of battle lifted from the South in 1865 it meant the end of the 'War Between the States,' but it marked the beginning of a new battle for the South—a battle for its very existence as a free people, for its sacred civilization and for the exercise of its rights which General Grant had recognized and so frankly admitted at Appomattox and which President Lincoln so emphatically reaffirmed when he declared of the Southern States:

" 'I shall treat them as if they had never been away.'

"Lincoln's intentions toward the South were honest and sincere, because they were in harmony with the fundamental principles of American civilization. The issues which had riven the two sections had been settled by the arbitrament of the sword and out of the fairness and brotherly love of his great heart he found it possible to welcome the men of the South back into the union as brothers whose misunderstandings had been adjusted.

"And the bullet that snuffed out the holy light of Lincoln's life struck down the most powerful friend the South and civilization had above the Mason and Dixon line, and made it possible for Stevens and his unscrupulous henchmen of South-haters to attempt to carry out their infamous program of establishing a negro empire in the South, and setting the heel of a brutal and despotic tyranny upon the necks of a helpless, defenseless, but a sovereign people."

In this connection Thomas Nelson Page, the celebrated author, says:

"The war between the states destroyed the institution of slavery, the dark years of the carpetbagger's domination well-nigh destroyed the South and Anglo-Saxon civilization, for after the sword came the canker worm and the enforcement of despotic intrigue.

"After the Confederate soldiers had laid down their arms and accepted their paroles in good faith, singly, in squads, many of them on foot, without a dollar in their pockets, they returned to their desolate homes and began anew to rebuild their vanished fortunes.

"In so far as the Confederate soldier was concerned the war was over; he had fought to the limit of his capacity for the cause he was convinced was right; the issue had been settled by the sword and he had accepted the results. The reins of government had again been placed in the hands of the best men of the South and the voices of the former Confederate army commanders again were heard in the halls of the National Congress. Little attention was paid by them to the mouthings of the 'bloodhounds of hate,' directed by Lust and Greed, who, in peacetime, still refused to leave the track of their infamous conquest for spoils.

"For over a year peace ostensibly was hovering over the still smouldering battlefields of the South, but soon the thunder of the impending storm of Reconstruction was heard in the land. Throughout the North, and especially in New England, meetings were held and from pulpits, rostrums and public halls enemies of the South preached a crusade of extermination against the Southern people.

"If Grant's order to Halleck to 'eat out Virginia clear and clean so that crows flying over it will have, for the balance of the season, to carry their provender with them,' or his order to Sheridan to hang without trial any of Mosby's men who were caught, may be excused on the grounds that they were justified by the exigencies of war, what excuse is to be made for this tirade delivered after the war was over by Wendell Phillips from the pulpit of Henry Ward Beecher's church:

" 'I do not believe in battles ending this war. You may plant a fort in every district of the South, you may take possession of her capitals and hold them with your armies, but you have not begun to subdue her people. I know it means something like absolute barbarian conquest, I allow it, but I do not believe there will be any peace until 347,-000 men of the South are either hanged or exiled.'

"And this, some time later, from 'Parson' Brownlow, ex-governor of Tennessee, at a convention held in New York:

" 'If I had the power I would arm every wolf, panther, catamount and bear in the mountains of America, every crocodile in the swamps of Florida, every negro in the South, every devil in hell, clothe them in the uniform of the Federal army and turn them loose on the rebels of the South and exterminate every man, woman and child south of Mason and Dixon's line. I would like to see negro troops, under the command of Butler, crowd every rebel into the Gulf of Mexico and drown them as the devil did the hogs in the Sea of Galilee.'

"In another convention held in Philadelphia 'Parson' Brownlow said:

" 'I am one of those who believe the war ended too soon. We have whipped the South, but not enough. The loyal masses constitute an overwhelming majority of the people of this country and they intend to march again on the South and intend this second war shall be no child's play. The second army will, as they ought to, make the entire South as God found the earth—without form and void.'

"Following Brownlow's speech Governor Yates, of Illinois, rose in his seat and said:

" 'Illinois furnished 250,000 troops to fight the South, and now we are ready to furnish 500,000 more to finish the good work.'

"And who was this Butler that 'Parson' Brownlow wished to command an army of negro troops and drive every former Confederate soldier into the Gulf of Mexico? It was Butler who ordered General Weitzel to compel the negroes of La Fourche Parish, Louisiana, to murder the white people of the parish. In reply to this order General Weitzel wrote:

" 'The idea of my inciting a negro insurrection is heartrending. I will resign my command rather than induce negroes to outrage and murder the helpless whites.'

"Indicating the storm of hate let loose upon the South after the Civil War and for the purpose of disclosing what our histories gloss over—that the people of the South were compelled to fight a second war more terrible than the first to preserve their honor and the land of their birth, the former facts compiled by Lamar Fontaine, C.E., Ph.D., of Lyons, Miss., who lived through that perilous period, are reproduced:

" 'Thus it was that for two years after the close of the great war in every hamlet and convention hall in the North thousands of preachers, orators and teachers dinned into the ears of the listening multitudes their fiendish venom until a wild wave of fanatical, insane New England Puritan hate swept like an East Indian hurricane over the entire North. . . . The Southern members of the National Congress were impotent to stay the dark whirlwind of hate as a cork floating upon the crest of a tidal wave. Then a species of negro insanity raged among the negrophiles of the New England states and it too spread like a prairie fire and took possession of the unthinking masses. Books and pamphlets fell from the New England presses like hail from a passing cloud. Men and women, from pulpit and rostrum, advocated the mixing of the negro and the white races and the establishment of a negro republic in the South after its conquered people had first been destroyed and the land rendered, as Parson Brownlow expressed, 'as God found it, without form and void.'

"Judge Salmon P. Chase, member of Lincoln's cabinet, paid a visit to the South after the surrender. Returning home, he said:

" 'I found the whites a worn-out, effete race, without vigor, mental or physical. On the contrary the negroes are alive, alert, full of energy. I predict in 25 years the negroes of the South will be at the head of all affairs, political, religious, the arts and sciences.'

"Henry Ward Beecher asserted:

" 'The negro is superior to the white race. If the latter do not forget their pride of race and color and amalgamate with the purer and richer blood of the blacks they will die out and wither away in unprolific skinniness.'

"The spread of the anti-Southern sentiment throughout the North forced Congress to act and the Reconstruction Act was the result. Southern senators and representatives were sent back to their homes, the entire civil government of the South was disrupted, and the negro was placed in power in every department, state and national. In support of this Reconstruction Act in Congress, James A. Garfield, former Major General in the Union Army, later elected President of the United States, said:

" 'This act set out by laying hands on all the rebel state governments and taking the very breath of life out of them. In the next place it puts a bayonet at the breast of every rebel in the South. In the next it leaves in the hands of Congress utter and absolute power over the people of the South.' "

NATHAN BEDFORD FORREST

A rare photograph of Grand Wizard Forrest, taken about
1869, in Memphis, Tenn., then his home.

Founder and first Imperial Wizard of the Knights of the Ku
Klux Klan immediately after the Civil War of 1861-1865.

Lieutenant General in the Confederate States Armies and considered by military historians one of the greatest cavalry commanders of all time. (See Appendix C.)

CHAPTER XIII

RECONSTRUCTION A TRAGEDY

"The Reconstruction acts of Congress constitute the most appalling tragedy in human history. Elections in the South were carried at the point of the bayonet, white men of the South were forced away from the polls and negroes and conscienceless carpetbaggers from the North, who had been in the South only a few weeks, were allowed to cast ballots and were elected to office. All in violation of our Constitution and every fundamental principle of Republican government.

"These carpetbaggers and their unscrupulous associates in the North were NOT the valiant soldiers who fought and bled on the battlefields, but, using a modern phrase, they were the cowardly 'slackers' of that time, pie-counter politicians and unreasonable and unreasoning fanatics.

"Constitutional law was stripped by profane hands of her virtuous vestments; ignorance, lust and hate seized the reins of state; the long-established order of society was disrupted by the sudden elevation to power of a grossly inferior race, led by fiends in human form, and the very blood of the Caucasian race was threatened with an everlasting contamination.

"The whole land was fastened in the crushing jaws of a ruthless tyranny enthroned by military despotism; law and order, peace and justice were things of the past and that sacred bulwark of human liberty—the Constitution of the United States of America—was in practice considered a 'mere scrap of paper.' The originators and perpetrators of this, the darkest epoch in the history of the world, were NOT the good people of the North because they were in ignorance of the real facts of what was being done; carpetbag leaders responsible for this unparalleled reign of ruthless despotism were less than a dozen unscrupulous politicians, prompted by hate and led on in their infamous purpose by graft and greed, assisted by horders of Northern scoundrels.

"The chastity of wife, mother, daughter and sister was imperiled; life and living were made intolerable. In the name of the Law the property of the husband and father was ruthlessly snatched from him without provocation and confiscated and the grim visages of Want, Hunger, Fear and Woe unutterable were visible everywhere.

"The people of the South turned appealingly to the power of their national government, but were spurned away with contempt and scorn.

"But the cry of that defenseless, terrorized and bleeding people, scorned by their own government to which they had sworn renewed allegiance and by which they had been guaranteed protection, and with the treaty of peace signed by Grant and Lee branded by Stevens, in conduct if not in words, as a 'scrap of paper,' was not to go unanswered.

"The men who for four years had borne upon their

98

bayonets the Ark of the Confederacy, and who had seen their battle flags victorious on scenes of bloody fields, through one of the most savage wars in all history, heard and answered the cry, and, as Knights of the Invisible Empire, impelled by an instinct of the race, they leaped into the saddle, consecrated to their task by the touch of the hot tears of defenseless womanhood and borne upon the backs of their faithful steeds, they came, they saw, they conquered!

"From over the mysterious borderland, from the Empire of the Soul, the Ku Klux came. Out of the sable shadows of the darkest night that ever afflicted any people they rode with a determined purpose; pure, as typified by the snowy white of their ghostly garments; hearts loyal as ever pulsated, as typified by the cross on the crimson shield worn upon their manly breasts; and a sacred devotion that laughed at death and faltered not at danger, as typified by the sacrificial cross of the Christ.

"With the fiery cross, symbol of the purest and most loyal patriotism, as their beacon, the Ku Klux rode forth in the cause of humanity, to save the God-given heritage of racial integrity, restore civilization, protect the defenseless, shield that which was sacred, avenge the crimes against the innocent and to restore to a free-born people their sacred birthright created for them by the shed blood of a noble ancestry.

"Through the darkness of Reconstruction's night the Ku Klux rode, dispelled the darkness of that frightful night, and at the dawning of a glorious day they saw the shades of that frightful night receding. Right had been by them established over Might; the voice of music was heard again in the land, their purpose and mission were ended, they laid aside their spotless robes and the noblest order of real chivalry in the great world's history disbanded—the Ku Klux of yesterday rode no more.

"In spite of the noble purpose of the Ku Klux Klan and in spite of the great service it rendered to both the white and the negro races, to North as well as South, yes, to ALL America, no organization in the history of man ever had heaped upon it the abuse and misrepresentation that fell to its lot. Foes of the South and enemies of the Southern people viciously assailed it as a band of murderers who stopped at nothing, and who whipped and terrorized both black and white and vented its spite and avenged personal wrongs, real or fancied, upon whoever incurred its displeasure.

"No fouler slander ever was perpetrated. Instead of being murderers and cutthroats the members of the Ku Klux Klan were men of the highest type as a body and they were sworn to and stood firmly upon the sacred principles of constitutional law. They worked to safeguard life and property, or what there was left of it; to ameliorate the terrible conditions growing out of the presence of the carpetbaggers from the North and the scalawags from the South, who turned traitor to their own people, and their baneful influence over the negro.

"The Ku Klux of the Reconstruction period was the outgrowth of a dire necessity born of insufferable conditions forced on the Southern people by a group of greedy, conscienceless politicians, and the character of the men who were at its head in the various Southern states is a lasting rebuke to the charge that it was composed of a band of outlaws.

"Contrary to popular opinion the Ku Klux Klan was not sectional except as to territory. Among its members were many men who had fought in the Federal army and who had decided to make their homes in the South after the war. They held no resentment against their Southern brothers, they realized the insanity of attempting to force negro domination upon the South and they cast their lot with their former foes of the battlefield in the movement to restore the South to its rightful place in the nation.

"In addition to these many of the white soldiers of the Federal army of occupation who were actually on duty in the South and who were under orders to kill a member of the Invisible Empire on sight, were members of the Ku Klux Klan. And connected with the Klan work were hundreds of negroes who rendered a service of imperishable value and who suffered torture, and many death, at the hands of the Union League and the carpetbaggers for their unshakable fidelity.

"We have said that the Ku Klux spirit throughout the ages has been the anthithesis of tyranny, the foe of despotism, and always has fostered liberty. Why should we call it the Ku Klux spirit rather than by any other name, and why should we feel warranted in the assertion that it is the anthithesis of tyranny?

"The answer is found in the fact that men—especially men of the Anglo-Saxon race—have never submitted passively to oppression; his is an unconquered and unconquerable race. No matter how firmly the yoke was fixed about his neck, no matter how sharp was the cut of the lash upon his back, no matter how remote were his chances of securing his liberty, sooner or later he always has rebelled. Sooner or later his hands were at the throat of the tyrant and even though he failed and death was his portion he has died gladly rather than purchase life at the price of chains and slavery. Tyranny of the most heartless type, despotism of the most devilish nature and to the highest and most powerful degree were established upon the ruined South. Never before was there such conscienceless conduct towards any people. The people of the South were of and belonged to that 'unconquered race.' In the Reconstruction period tyranny reached its greatest height, and to successfully combat it in the interest of the blood-bought human rights of a sovereign people, that spirit which through the ages has always stood — 'the anthithesis of tyranny' — as at other times, asserted itself as never before. It flamed in human breasts, men united in organized form, an instrument of salvation, and the body, vitalized by this spirit, was called the Ku Klux Klan.

"Wherever and whenever oppression has prevailed that spirit of resentment, of determination to resist until the shackles are broken always has been found. So has it been always, is today and will be forever.

"Sometimes it has smouldered in secret for years and then flashed up at the psychological moment to ignite a world. Call it by whatever name you will, the spirit of rebellion against tyranny—the spirit of the followers of Calvin and Luther and Cromwell, of the Revolutionary fathers, of the Ku Klux of the Reconstruction period— is indestructible, and the man in whose breast that spirit lives will never submit to domination, social, religious or political, by any man or race of men, and will never acquiesce in the rule of injustice or a reign of wrong.

"The Ku Klux spirit has never manifested itself with force except when driven to it by the usurpation of power or attempt to usurp it. It has never questioned the right of any man of any race to live his life and conduct his own affairs as he sees fit so long as such conduct does not conflict with the established order of society.

"The Anglo-Saxon race, the only race that has ever proved its ability and supremacy and demonstrated its determination to progress under any and all conditions and handicaps, owes its high place in the world today to the fact that this spirit has been kept alive from the foundation of the world and has never lagged in any land or clime.

"And if the Anglo-Saxon race is to maintain its prestige, if it is to continue as the leader in the affairs of the world and to fulfill its sacred mission, it must maintain and jealously guard its purity, its power and its dignity, and while it should aid and encourage to the limit of its ability all men of whatever race or creed, it must forever maintain its own peculiar identity as the Anglo-Saxon race and preserve the integrity of its civilization, for the shores of Time hold the shipwreck of all the mongrel civilization of the past which is evidence that in keeping with the laws of creative justice Nature has decreed that mixed civilizations, together with governments of mixed races, are doomed to destruction and oblivion.

"From the past the voice of the great Lincoln must be heard:

" 'There are physical differences between the races which would forever forbid them living together on terms of political and social equality.'

"The imperative call of higher justice to the real patriots of our nation is:

"In the name of our valiant and venerated dead and in due respect to their stainless memory, and in the interest of peace and security of all peoples now living and for the sake of all those yet to be, keep Anglo - Saxon American civilization, institutions, politics and society pure and thereby, since we have received this sacred heritage, transmit it with clean hands and pure hearts to generations yet unborn; thereby keeping faith with the mind, soul and purpose of our valiant sires and transmit our name into the future without dishonor and without disgrace.

"Let the solemn behest of higher duty be promptly and properly met in all the relationships of life and living without fault, without fail, without fear and without reproach, now and forevermore.

"The Ku Klux may be antagonized and forced to fight many battles, but perish, never! To destroy it is an impossibility, for it belongs in essence to the realms spiritual. It is unshaken by unjust criticisms, no power can thwart it in its onward conquest of right; it courts not the plaudits of the populace, nor is it swerved from its course by the libel of its foes. Attuned with Deity, functioning only for all humanity's good, misjudged by ignorance, misunderstood by many, slandered by prejudice, sweeping on under the divine leadership of duty, it never falters and will never fail.

The spirit of the Ku Klux Klan still lives, and should live, a priceless heritage to be sacredly treasured by all those who love our country (regardless of section) and are proud of its sacred traditions. That this spirit may live always to warm the hearts of manly men, unify them by the force of a holy clannishness, to assuage the billowing tide of fraternal alienation that surges in human breasts, and inspire them to achieve the highest and noblest in the defense of our country, our homes, humanity and each other, is the paramount ideal of the Knights of the Ku Klux Klan.

"The Klan, growing fast in numbers, influence, and power, and standing for a 100 per cent Americanism, devoted to the purest principles of patriotism, as well as to charity and fraternalism, has been attacked by forces represented by the Catholic Church, the negroes, and the Jews. We have no quarrel and are not opposed to these sects or races. They, however, are the forces behind the investigation by the House of Representatives Rules Committee.[1] At this hearing nothing was developed that could possibly be construed concerning the Knights of the Ku Klux Klan as derogatory to our great organization. At the hearing we repeatedly urged the Rules Committee to order a full investigation by a special Congressional Committee. No action was taken by the committee, which is ample evidence that the investigation revealed nothing in the history, actions, and records of the Klan contrary to any accepted American standard of management for fraternal orders. We do not fear the light on any of our actions, and we welcome at all times the fullest possible investigation into our principles and our work for the Republic.

"It is true we bar from membership Jews, Catholics, and negroes. These classes also bar from membership in their organizations persons who are not Jews, Catholics, or Negroes. We have that same right. We do not deny that we are strictly a Protestant and American fraternal order, which is destined to be the greatest brotherly and patriotic organization in the wide world."

---

[1] The second Congressional investigation of the Klan in 1921.

JUDGE PAUL S. ETHERIDGE
One of the founders of the new Klan and for many years its
general councillor and chief attorney.

107

CHAPTER XIV

THE KU KLUX KLAN UNDER
IMPERIAL WIZARD SIMMONS

Associated with Colonel Simmons in the supreme office of the Knights of the Ku Klux Klan, at the Imperial Palace in Atlanta, were some of the most prominent citizens of Georgia. Next in authority to Colonel Simmons and the chief moving force of the Knights of the Ku Klux Klan was Edward Young Clarke,[1] of Atlanta.

Mr. Clarke was a young man of tremendous energy and large experience. He was Chief of Staff of the "Imperial Wizard" and his official title was "Imperial Kleagle." Mr. Clarke, in association with Mrs. Elizabeth Tyler, had conducted for many years the Southern Publicity Association in Atlanta. This was an advertising and publicity company and was the largest organization of its kind in the South.

Among other work of a public character that it had performed had been the conduct of various "drives" of a patriotic and humanitarian kind. It had conducted money raising campaigns at various times, at which it has been remarkably successful, for the Anti-Saloon League, the

---

[1] and [2] Not now connected with or employed by the Klan. Mrs. Tyler is deceased.

Salvation Army, and other national organizations. Whenever big organizations in the South desired to launch public movements of various kinds, so well known was the Southern Publicity Association, and so national in scope its reputation, that this organization was nearly always the first to be approached to take charge of such movements. Mr. Clarke was by profession a newspaperman, and one of the most experienced and able publicity directors in the South. He came of an excellent Southern family. His brother was managing editor of the Atlanta Constitution, one of the greatest and best known Southern newspapers. His business partner, Mrs. Elizabeth Tyler, was a remarkable woman.[2] She was in active charge of the affairs of the Southern Publicity Association. At the age of 14 Mrs. Tyler was uneducted. She was left a widow with one child at the age of 15, and she then could barely read or write. In many ways she acquired a fair education, but her real education was obtained in large business affairs with which she had been connected.

Mrs. Tyler had at the beginning no connection with the Ku Klux Klan, as women were not then admitted to membership in that organization. The Southern Publicity Association was used as a valuable adjunct to the Department of Propagation of the Klan, and it was largely due to the ability and experience of Mr. Clarke and Mrs. Tyler in great publicity campaigns that the organization grew rapidly.

"Now," said Mr. Clarke, in an interview, "I want to tell you what the Ku Klux organization stands for. First and foremost, the real 100 per cent American needs to be

109

baptized in the faith of our forefathers. In the strenuous rush of the big business of this nation we have forgotten the spirit which came from around that table where sat the real men who planned for this great nation. We say that a revival in spirit of real Americanism must start first in the hearts, minds, and souls of the 100 per cent Americans; and we are getting these men together and getting them into this organization. When we get them in, we propose to rebaptize them in the spirit of Americanism under the Stars and Stripes, and in the ideals of the men who founded this nation and upon whose ideals and plans it has grown so great.

"We are building a fellowship, a great social, compact body. We have drawn a tight line and propose to build a great reservoir of real Americanism.

"White supremacy—I am not afraid of that word— for I can go into a colored meeting anywhere and talk to them about it; it has been misused and misrepresented by the enemies of both races who for various reasons want to see trouble started; the enemies of real Americans who want to see America manacled, who want to see a polluted America instead of the America which has been handed down to us by our forefathers.

"The foreign element in America is attempting to get control of the reins of government.

"Statements that the Klan has fomented lynchings or race riots are lies. In not a single place where a Klan is organized and in full operation has a race riot or lynching occurred. The Klan stands for all that is great and

110

good in our civilization, and it will exist as long as the United States endures.

"The organization now has approximately 1,500 chartered Klans, and the total membership of these Klans is more than 100,000 members actually initiated.[1] The organization has approximately one hundred thousand applications of persons desirous of becoming members, who are being investigated and whose applications will be acted upon within the next 60 days. Approximately 1,000 members per day are now being taken in by the organization. Since the attack of the New York newspapers, and the hearing before the Congressional Committee, applications for membership have increased 20 per cent above the normal average for six months previous to the beginning of the attacks on the Klan. In order not to take in undesirable persons, as a result of the interest and intensity of feeling aroused throughout the country, the organization is using extra precautions regarding the new members and instead of holding an application three weeks previous to acting upon it, as has been the custom, instructions have gone out for all applications to be held 60 days previous to being acted upon, hoping through this method to eliminate from the applicants any person who might be applying for membership simply out of curiosity, or through a certain enthusiasm along religious or racial lines.

---

[1] January 1, 1922.

"The Klan is now actively operating in 45 states and has a King Kleagle, or state manager, in 41 states. The state managers have under them approximately six hundred Kleagles or organizers. The nation is divided into nine groups known as 'Domains,' with a Director General in these groups carrying the title of 'Grand Goblin.' The nine 'Grand Goblins' are located in the cities of Boston, New York, Philadelphia, Washington, Chicago, Atlanta, St. Louis, Houston, and Los Angeles. The organization is now seriously considering the elimination of the fee system, or commission basis in the Department of Propagation, and contemplates placing the Grand Goblins, King Kleagles, and Kleagles on a straight salary basis. (This was done later).

"The Department of Propagation is a separate division of the work from the ritualistic activities of the Knights of the Ku Klux Klan. The Department of Propagation is charged with the duty of organizing new Klans in places where Klans of the organization have not previously existed, and when these Klans are organized they are turned over to the Invisible Empire to be chartered. After being chartered the Department of Propagation has no further interest in or connection with that particular Klan. New Klans are chartered on the numerical basis of approximately one-third of the possible total membership of the Klan in any local community, but the average number chartered within the past six months has been approximately on a basis of one-fourth the approximate final total membership in any one community.

"After being chartered the local Klan retains one-half of the fee or klectokon,[1] or donation paid by members on entering the organization, and the other half is sent to the Imperial Palace, and goes into the treasury of the organization for the general use of the organization in its work.

"The principles of the Knights of the Ku Klux Klan, as announced in all the publications and rituals of the organization, are as follows:

"The purpose of the modern Ku Klux Klan is to inculcate the sacred principles and noble ideals of chivalry, the development of character, the protection of the home and the chastity of womanhood, the exemplification of a pure and practical patriotism toward our glorious country, the preservation of American ideals and institutions, and the maintenance of white supremacy.

"No man is admitted to the fellowship of the Invisible Empire of today who hasn't manhood enough to assume a real oath to Right and Duty with serious purpose to keep the same inviolate. No man is admitted to fellowship who will not, or who cannot swear an unqualified allegiance to the Government of the United States of America, its flag, its Constitution and its institutions.

"Only native-born white American citizens, who believe in the tenets of the Christian religion, and who owe no allegiance of any degree or nature to any foreign government or institution, religious or political, or to any sect, people, or persons, are eligible for membership.

---

[1] $10 initiation fee.

113

"While its name would indicate it is purely a Southern organization such is not the case. It is non-sectional, non-political, and non-sectarian. It is a purely patriotic, fraternal organization. In fact, the organization, in the six years of its existence, already has numbered among its membership many men, some of them nationally known, who have never lived in the South. As proof of its non-political attitude men prominent in both Democratic and Republican parties, including members of Congress, are leaders in the organization. Its compelling appeal to citizens of all sections lies in the fact that it is strictly an institution of, by, and for white citizens of the United States, pledged to fundamental Amreican ideals and institutions.

"While membership in the Ku Klux Klan is open only to white American citizens the organization wages war on no individual or organization regardless of race, color, or creed. It takes no part as an organization in any political or religious controversy, and it concedes the right of every man to think, vote, and worship God as he pleases.

"Because certain individuals at various times have committed acts of violence under cover of darkness, and shielded by masks and robes resembling the official regalia of the Ku Klux Klan, they have been classed as members of this organization. The Ku Klux Klan is a strictly law-abiding organization and every member is sworn to uphold the law at all times, and to assist officers of the law in preserving peace and order whenever the occasion may arise. Any member violating this oath would be banished

114

forever from the organization. In other words, it is a practical fraternal order pledged to wholesome service, and not merely a social association.

"Among the principles for which this organization stands, in addition to those already enumerated, are: Suppression of graft by public officeholders; preventing unwarranted strikes by foreign agitators; preventing the causes of mob violence and lynchings; sensible and patriotic immigration laws; sovereignty of state rights under the Constitution; separation of Church and State, freedom of speech and press, a freedom of such that does not strike at or imperil our Government or the cherished institutions of our people.

"If there be any white American citizen who owes allegiance to any flag but the Star Spangled Banner, and who cannot subscribe to and support these principles, let him forever hold his peace. He is basely unworthy of the great Flag and its Government that guarantees to him life, liberty, and the pursuit of happiness. That person who actively opposes these great principles is a dangerous ingredient in the body politic of our country, and an enemy to the weal of our national commonwealth.

"The Ku Klux Klan of today rides on, not upon the backs of faithful steeds but in the mind, heart, and soul of every true white American citizen who loves our great country and who glories in the name American, and who is honest enough as a grateful son to perpetually memorialize the heroism of our fathers and transmit the boon of our priceless heritage untarnished, uncorrupted, and unstained to the generations who follow us, that the lustre

115

of our age may increase in splendor. For he who forgets the heroes of the past is basely unworthy of the blessings of the present, and he should be forgotten by posterity."

Under Simmons the following were the first officers of the Klan:

H. C. Montgomery, "Imperial Treasurer" of the Knights of the Ku Klux Klan, was one of Atlanta's prominent business men. He owned a large optical store in Atlanta, was a graduate of the Northern School of Optometry in Chicago, and had followed his profession for many years.

He was a native of Kentucky, but had lived in Atlanta for many years, where he had a reputation for integrity and fair business dealing. He had been a steward in the Methodist Church for some years, and was a member of Atlanta Commandery No. 9, Knights Templar. He had been associated with the Klan since its foundation in 1915.

Though then owning a large and prosperous business in Atlanta Mr. Montgomery devoted practically all his time to the affairs of the Klan.

"The Knights of the Ku Klux Klan are bound together in a great law-abiding, patriotic American organization," said Mr. Montgomery. "I shall continue my connection with it as long as I am of use to it."

The "Imperial Klonsel," or supreme attorney, was Paul S. Etheridge, now a Superior Court Judge of Fulton County, Georgia. He is a native of Greensboro, Georgia; was educated at Mercer University. He began the practice of law in Atlanta and is recognized as one of the leading lawyers of the Atlanta Bar. He is a deacon in the

Baptist Church. In 1918 he was elected a member of the Board of Commissioners of Roads and Revenues in Fulton County, Georgia, in which Atlanta is located, and was chairman of that board. No citizen of Atlanta has a higher standing in the public estimation than Judge Etheridge.

"The Ku Klux Klan," said Mr. Etheridge, "is a righteous and great organization, standing for all of that which is best in our civilization; it stands for righteousness and the right in everything and abhors lawlessness and crime."

Louis David Wade, "Imperial Secretary," was a native of Oswego, New York. He moved to Atlanta when fifteen years old and for many years was connected with the Southern Bell Telephone and Telegraph Company, with which corporation he had a fine record. Later he was superintendent of cotton mills at Cedartown, Georgia; Bowling Green, North Carolina; and Greenville, North Carolina. For some time he was superintendent of the municipal electric light plant at Greenville, North Carolina. He was a member of the Methodist Church, and belonged to a number of secret orders. Mr. Wade had an excellent reputation in Atlanta.

"The Knights of the Ku Klux Klan," said Mr. Wade, "are animated with good purpose. The organization is founded upon right principles. Its business affairs are conducted with honest, straightforward dealings; it is destined to be the greatest order of patriotic Americans in this country, and it will become, in time, the greatest fraternal organization in the whole world. I am proud to be an officer in such an organization."

117

F. L. Savage, "Grand Goblin," who was head of the Department of Investigation of the Knights of the Ku Klux Klan, is a native of Boston, Massachusetts. He is one of the most experienced and capable detectives in the United States. For thirteen years he was head of the Savage Detective Agency, in New York City. He served on transports during the Spanish-American War, and during the World War was connected with the Railroad Administration.

In 1921 Mr. Savage was brought from New York to Atlanta, to head the Investigation Department of the Klan. He organized one of the most active departments of the Klan. The scope of the Investigation Department was large and important.

"Our biggest problem," said Mr. Savage, "is those who commit crimes of various kinds in widely separated sections, and charge them to the Klan. Cowardly acts are committed, laws violated, and often the scoundrels who perpetrate these acts cover them with the name of the Klan. It is part of our work to refute these charges and to investigate practices of this nature. For instance, if a Klan is charged with tarring, feathering, and whipping a victim anywhere, we immediately dispatch investigators to the scene of the crime, and if we find that even one member of a local Klan has been guilty of such outrages, summary action is taken. The Imperial Palace immediately cancels the charter of that whole Klan, and we do everything in our power to aid the prosecuting attorney and the officers of justice to arrest the guilty and bring them to trial.

"Our organization abhors every unlawful action of every kind, but occasionally a man of bad intentions secures membership in the Klan, and it is a few of these persons who have caused on occasions charges against the Klan. Our investigations have shown that on many occasions outrages and crimes of many kinds perpetrated in the South and North, and charged to the Klan or Klansmen, were done by persons who had no connection whatever with the Klan.

"The Knights of the Ku Klux Klan are a law-abiding organization, and they are utterly opposed to any violation of the law at any time. We shall never tolerate in our membership any person who violates any law.

"Already we have assisted in bringing to justice persons who have impersonated Klansmen and perpetrated crimes of various kinds. Our Investigation Department reaches into every state."

HONORABLE HUGO BLACK
Associate Justice of the United States Supreme Court. Once
the most prominent Klansman in his native State of Alabama.
Photograph by Underwood & Underwood.

120

CHAPTER XV

VARIED ACTIVITIES OF THE KLAN

Part of the work of the Ku Klux is charitable. It also interests itself in civic welfare work of many kinds. For instance, September 24, 1920, the Chamber of Commerce of Yoakum, Texas, accepted an offer of the Yoakum Klan to loan $30,000 to the city for erection and equipment of a public library. It was stipulated in the loan by the Klan that six Holy Bibles must be on file in the library, and the Stars and Stripes must fly at all times over the building.

On September 17[1] in Richmond, Virginia, a police officer was killed by a desperado. The Richmond Klan sent $100 to the widow.

Charleston, West Virginia, Klansmen on August 27 contributed $275 toward the support of the Old Ladies' Home in Kanawha County.

Last March the Charlottesville, Virginia, Klan gave $1,000 to the University of Virginia Centennial Endowment Fund.

November 24, the Henderson, Texas, Klan gave $50 to two negroes in needy circumstances.

---

[1] The following dates are all in 1920 or 1921.

October 1, the Atlanta Klan contributed $100 to help pay expenses of Confederate veterans from Atlanta to Houston, Texas, at the annual reunion of the United Confederate Veterans.

November 23, the Greenville, Texas, Klan contributed $1,000 toward rebuilding Wesley College at that place, destroyed by fire.

On Christmas Day, 1921, the Atlanta Ku Klux Klan contributed $125 to the Christmas fund for former slaves.

November 25 the Memphis, Tennessee, Klan gave $100 to the Red Cross.

On November 7, the Goliad, Texas, Klan contributed $50 to a citizen of that town whose home and personal effects had been destroyed by fire.

On June 22 last the San Antonio, Texas, Klan gave $100 to the local Orphan's Home.

On July 6, the Wharton, Texas, Klan contributed $50 to a widow in destitute circumstances.

On July 9, the Cuero, Texas, Klan gave County Judge Boal $60 to help a man afflicted with tuberculosis.

On November 21, the Austin, Texas, Klan gave $100 to the Salvation Army.

On July 20, the Dallas, Texas, Klan sent $100 to the Orphans' Home.

The Atlanta Klan contributed $1,000 to Agnes Scott College in that city.

The Washington, D. C., Klan gave $100 to the Salvation Army.

More than $15,000 has been loaned by the Atlanta Klan to small tradesmen who need capital in their business.

This money is supplied without interest. In many other cities where there are large Klans many thousands of dollars are loaned to small tradesmen.

It is one of the cardinal principles of the Klan to assist each other in all business and social affairs, and a Klansman will always trade with other Klansmen whenever possible. This same policy is often pursued, as is well known, by other fraternal organizations.

The Klans everywhere are opposed to lawlessness and disorder. As organizations they are always ready to assist local civil officers with money or advice. For instance, on May 19,[1] the South Jacksonville, Florida, Klan sent a communication to Mayor William Beloit to the effect that they stood back of him in his efforts to preserve law and order in that community. There had recently been considerable disorder in South Jacksonville, and criminals of various kinds had been giving the authorities much trouble.

Last January at Winter Garden,[1] Florida, there was a race riot. The local Klansmen helped to suppress the riot, and members of that Klan stood guard for three days and three nights, protecting lives and property in the negro quarters.

On February 25, 1921, D. J. Gantt, Federal Supervising Prohibition Agent for the Southern States, stated in writing:

"I feel that I have the support of the Knights of the Ku Klux Klan in supporting my part of the law — the prohibition part."

---

[1] (All 1921).

123

J. L. Couch, Mayor of Columbus, Georgia, in an open statement on February 5, 1921, highly praised the Columbus Klan. He said:

"Seventeen members of the Klan assisted the police department during an epidemic of burglaries and their services were appreciated by the police and myself. An organization like the Ku Klux Klan is a blessing to any community."

In Atlanta a mob formed in the streets to storm the jail and lynch a negro charged with an atrocious crime. Colonel Simmons happened to be passing and sent members of the Klan among the mob to persuade them to disband, which was done. Later when the negro was carried from the jail to the courthouse to be tried Klansmen stationed along the way between the two buildings prevented any act of violence against the accused.

The Little Rock, Ark., chief of police received November 25,[1] $1,000 from the Klan at that place, as a reward for the arrest and conviction of any person attacking a woman. Many of the local Klans have adopted the motto: "Not for self but for others."

As for charges against the Klan that it is hostile to the Catholics, Jews, and the negroes, Colonel Simmons gave the author the following written statement:

"We antagonize no man's religion. I have heard of only one case where a Kleagle circulated anti-Catholic propaganda and he was instantly discharged.

"We are not anti-Jewish; any Jew who can subscribe to the tenets of the Christian Religion can get in.

---

[1] 1921.

124

"We are not anti-negro. Scores of other fraternal organizations do not admit negroes. We are not anti-foreign born, we merely require that members shall be native born Americans."

Colonel Simmons stated the prerequisites to membership in the Invisible Empire as follows:

"This Order is founded upon dependable character. It is not an ultra-exclusive institution, but its membership is composed of 'picked men.'

"No man is wanted in the Order who has not manhood enough to assume a real oath with serious purpose of keeping the same inviolate.

"No man is wanted in this Order who will not or cannot swear an unqualified allegiance to the Government of the United States of America, its flag and its Constitution.

"No man is wanted in this Order who does not esteem the Government of the United States above any other government, civil, political, or ecclesiastical, in the whole world.

"No man is wanted in this Order who cannot practice fraternity toward each other and every one of his oath-bound associates.

"Only native-born Americans who believe in the tenets of the Christian religion and who owe no allegiance of any degree or nature to any foreign government, nation, institution, sect, people or person, are eligible."

In Atlanta, the Klan's headquarters, practically the entire population believes in the Klan and one of the largest local Klans in the Invisible Empire[2] is located in this city, numbering many thousand members, including a large number of the most prominent citizens.

Practically the entire citizenship is back of it, and this fact alone, in its home city, seems evidence that the Klan must be a good and reputable organization.

An illustration of how the Klan is regarded in Atlanta is shown by a sermon delivered by Dr. Caleb A. Ridley,[1] then Pastor of the Central Baptist Church, one of the largest churches in Atlanta, in which the minister took occasion to criticize newspapers that had attacked the Klan, and made from the pulpit a vigorous defense of the organization. Dr. Ridley was one of the most prominent ministers in the South.

While the Invisible Empire then published no newspaper and had no propaganda or publicity department, it had use of the columns of the Searchlight, a weekly newspaper then printed in Atlanta, which was the official paper of the Junior Order of United American Mechanics for Georgia. The editor of this paper was J. O. Wood, and the managing editor Howard B. Weaver. It had a very large circulation throughout Georgia and elsewhere, and was at all times a vigorous defender of the Klan, though having no official connection with the "Invisible Empire." Some Georgia newspapers are favorable to the Klan; some are hostile. The Klan has recently established its own publication, the "Fiery Cross."

---

[2] There were (1939) 15 Klans in Atlanta.

[1] Deceased.

Parades of the Klan in their white regalia are always a big event in Atlanta. The first public appearance of the Klan on a large scale in Atlanta was during the Confederate Veterans' Reunion in 1919. The Ku Kluxers paraded clad in their helmets, masks, and long, flowing white robes, and created a stir along the line of march. They fellowed the veterans in the parade.

On January 16, 1920, Atlanta prohibitionists had a great bonfire in the center of the city, to celebrate the "dry amendment," which marked the death of John Barleycorn. The Klan on this occasion appeared again in uniform to emphasize the fact that it stands at all times for law and order, and for fair and impartial enforcement of all laws, not only of the prohibition law, but of all statutes.

Colonel Simmons summed up the central idea of the Ku Klux Klan, by saying:

"The spirit of the Ku Klux Klan still lives, and should live a priceless heritage to be sacredly treasured by all those who love their country, regardless of section, and are proud of its sacred traditions, That this spirit may live always to warm the hearts of manly men, unify them by the spirit of holy klannishness, and inspire them to highest ideals and noblest in the defense of our country, our homes, each other, and humanity, is the paramount ideal of the Knights of the Ku Klux Klan."

CHAPTER XVI

ENEMIES BEGIN ATTACKS ON THE KLAN

September, 1921, largely because of its intense activities and the enemies it had made among certain classes, the Klan began to be attacked in a few newspapers. The attack started with public statements, widely carried by the press services, by certain Kleagles, who had become disgruntled with their positions or who had otherwise been influenced to abandon their work and assail the organization.

The New York World began a "crusade" against the Klan and published a series of newspaper articles attacking the Klan and purporting to expose its secrets and describe its activities. The principal fact upon which the World based its attacks was the amount of initiation dues collected by the Klan, and its alleged participation in tarring and feathering cases which were charged against the Klan and which were afterward proven to have been perpetrated by persons not having any connection with the organization.

Whether or not the fact that the World[1] was principally owned by Joseph Pulitzer, a Jew, and his brother, had anything to do with the crusade, is not known, but the

[1] Now combined with the New York Telegram — the World-Telegram.

fact that Jews, as a rule, are ineligible to membership in the Klan, because they do not belong to the Christian religion, should be taken into consideration in a survey of this attack.

Another fact connected with the World's crusade that may bear on the situation is, that after the World began to publish the Knights of the Ku Klux Klan articles, its daily circulation increased approximately 100,000, and the Sunday circulation 125,000 copies, according to a statement published by the World in a New York trade journal.

It is a fact known by all newspaper publishers that the New York World had always been noted for "crusades" of various kinds, and had been the leading propaganda newspaper, advocating and opposing various things, for many years in New York City.

The New York World syndicated its Knights of the Ku Klux Klan articles and sold them to a considerable number of daily papers throughout the country for which, of course, it was paid. So from a money standpoint the attacks on the Klan were profitable to the World, aside from any questionable prestige it may have secured from the publication.

In the whole World series there is hardly a fact borne out by reliable testimony or evidence that the Klan had been guilty of any practice or any action contrary to the management of an ordinary fraternal organization. Those who read the World articles will agree that while they were sensational and entertainingly written, there was a scarcity of facts in the stories.

When it became known in New York that the World had gained more than 100,000 circulation because of the Knights of the Ku Klux Klan stories, and circulation in New York means advertising, and advertising means money, the New York American launched a similar attack on the "Invisible Empire," and used as its principal medium in its series of stories a former official of the Klan in New York, C. Anderson Wright, who had left the organization. The Hearst stories were printed in all the Hearst papers throughout the United States.

Publication by the World syndicate and in the Hearst string of newspapers, of course, secured very wide publicity for the attacks throughout the country, and while both series were being published Congress took notice of the matter, and after considerable private discussion among the members of the House a Congressional attack was launched on the Klan.

Resolutions were introduced calling on the House Rules Committee to hold a preliminary investigation to decide whether or not a special Congressional committee should make an investigation of the "Invisible Empire." These resolutions, practically similar in purpose, were introduced by Representative Peter F. Tague, of Boston, Massachusetts; Representative Leonidas C. Dyer, of St. Louis, Msisouri; and Representative Thomas J. Ryan, of New York City.

Representative James A. Gallivan, Democrat, of South Boston, later introduced a resolution calling for a Congressional committee to investigate and determine whether any members of Congress belonged to the Knights of the

Ku Klux Klan. This resolution was not taken seriously, for it was evident to any Washington newspaperman that Congress would never pass such a resolution.

Some observers professed to see considerable significance in the resolutions of Messrs. Tague and Ryan, as Mr. Ryan is a Catholic and a Knight of Columbus, and Mr. Tague also a Catholic. Representative Dyer is a Protestant, but had in his constituency in St. Louis, Missouri, a large number of negro voters.

Messrs. Dyer and Ryan are Republicans, but Mr. Tague is a Democrat. Mr. Tague lives in Boston, which has a large Catholic and foreign-born population. Mr. Ryan's home is in New York City, which possesses a very large Jewish, negro, and foreign-born population.

While few open comments were made concerning these facts during the investigation by the House Rules Committee, though Colonel Simmons called attention to it, the inference seemed to be plain that the House members who had introduced the resolution to investigate the Klan were prompted by personal and religious feelings, and it was evident to all that by their resolutions they had secured considerable political advantage in their congressional districts.

Representative William D. Upshaw, a Democrat of Georgia, soon after the Ryan, Tague and Dyer resolutions were launched, introduced a resolution calling upon Congress to investigate all secret societies in the United States. This created considerable stir throughout the country and further complicated the already tangled situation.

It was an open secret that several Southern congressmen had prepared resolutions demanding that Congress investigate the Knights of Columbus, and the various negro organizations throughout the Country, particularly the National Association for the Advancement of Colored People, headquarters in Boston. These congressmen had their resolutions ready, but were prevailed upon not to introduce the resolutions until it was seen what action the Rules Committee would take toward appointing a special congressional committee to probe the affairs of the "Invisible Empire." It was well known, however, that the Southern Democrats generally, in the House and Senate, had determined, if there was to be a special congressional investigation of the Ku Klux Klan, the House Rules Committee investigation being merely a preliminary proceeding as to whether or not a special congressional committee should investigate the Klan, to force a special congressional investigation of the Knights of Columbus and all negro organizations.

The result would have been a religious controversy in Congress that might have led to very serious consequences, and which undoubtedly would have split the United States into hostile factions. In view of all the circumstances it is well that the Southern congressmen did not introduce their resolutions. The threat of such resolutions, however, undoubtedly had the effect of causing the Rules Committee to finally take no action for appointment of a special investigation committee.

Finally the Rules Committee decided to hold the preliminary investigation to decide whether or not a special congressional committee should investigate the Klan.

The House Rules Committee included: Representatives Philip P. Campbell, Kansas; Bertrand H. Snell, New York; William A. Rodenberg, Illinois; Simeon D. Fess, Ohio; Aaron S. Kreider, Pennsylvania; Porter H. Dale, Vermont; Royal C. Johnson, South Dakota; and Thomas D. Schall, Minnesota, all Republicans. Edward W. Pou, North Carolina; Finis J. Garrett, Tennessee; James C. Cantrill, Kentucky; and Daniel J. Riordan, New York, were the Democratic members.

Some of the members of the committee did not appear at the hearing. The chairman, Mr. Campbell, and Representative Rodenberg, of Illinois, showed by their attitude and questions of the witnesses that they desired an investigation, and that they were, if not distinctly hostile, at least unfavorable to the "Invisible Empire." Other members occupied a noncommittal and fair attitude. Among the Democrats, Representative Pou and Representative Garrett indicated by their questions and their attitude during the whole hearing that they were not only anxious to bring out all the facts concerning the Ku Klux Klan, but that they were in a favorable frame of mind toward the organization. So far as known, none of the members of the House Rules Committee were members of the "Invisible Empire."

Mr. Campbell is a Protestant and so are Mr. Pou and Mr. Garrett, Mr. Rodenberg is also a Protestant.

The investigation of the House Rules Committee continued for several days, beginning on October 11, 1921.

133

Mr. Tague appeared and urged that the committee vote for a congressional investigation.

Mr. Dyer was the next witness and urged a favorable report on his resolution, as did Mr. Ryan.

Among the witnesses were Roland Thomas, member of the editorial staff of the New York World, who had charge, for the World, of the investigation of the Ku Klux Klan. Thomas said he had devoted July, August, and September to the investigation. He made this significant admission on the stand: "A great deal of what comes to it (referring to the World) has to come by rumor. I cannot pretend to go thoroughly to the bottom (referring to the investigation), for the very fact I have spoken of, that a newspaper has no power of subpoena or search."

The star witness, however, was C. Anderson Wright, formerly a member of the New York Klan with title of "King Kleagle," that is, he was in charge of the whole State of New York as manager. Wright's testimony, which occupied several of the hearings, was mainly devoted to statements regarding the financial affairs of the Klan and its business matters. Nothing was brought out by the former "King Kleagle" which could be considered as derogatory to the Klan; the principal burden of his testimony was that the Klan had collected "enormous sums of money." It was shown that the total revenues of the Klan since it had been organized six years before had been approximately $1,250,000. A financial statement as to how this money had been spent was filed with the

134

committee by Colonel Simmons, and there was nothing in the report which showed any misuse of funds. The money had been spent to pay organizers' commissions, rentals, printing, postage, and other usual expenses of a large fraternal organization.

CHAPTER XVII

MANY OTHER WITNESSES
BEFORE COMMITTEE

O. K. Williamson was the next witness. He is a post-office inspector who had made an investigation of the Klan. Mr. Williamson's testimony dealt largely with the purchase of the property owned by the Klan in Atlanta, and a home costing $25,000 in that city which had been purchased by members of the Klan and presented to Colonel Simmons.

Mr. Williamson also went thoroughly into the distribution of the funds donated by the Klan membership and largely covered the same ground as C. Anderson Wright.

Representative Gallivan, during the testimony by Mr. Williamson, asked the Rules Committee to favorably report his resolution to discover what members of Congress belonged to the Ku Klux Klan. It may authoritatively be stated that a large number of congressmen were then and now are members of the "Invisible Empire," just as many of them belong to the Masons, Elks, Odd Fellows, Knights of Pythias, Knights of Columbus, and other large fraternal organizations.

During the whole hearing William J. Burns, then Chief of the Bureau of Investigation, Department of

Justice, and Assistant United States Attorney General Crimm, with their assistants, occupied seats near the witness stand and closely observed everything. Mr. Crimm had been delegated by the Department of Justice to investigate the "Invisible Empire," and Mr. Burns had been for some time actively engaged in investigating the organization.

Judge Paul S. Etheridge, of Atlanta, Georgia, the Supreme Attorney for the Ku Klux Klan, was an important witness. He made out a strong case for the Klan and all its activities.

Representative William D. Upshaw, of Georgia, was also on the stand and paid a glowing tribute to the character and personal record of Colonel Simmons. He declared: "That as a sturdy and inspiring personality, as an heroic veteran of the Spanish-American War, and a Knight Templar, as a consecrated Christian, as a member of a dozen well-known fraternal organizations and a God-fearing citizen, Colonel Simmons is as incapable of an unworthy or unpatriotic motive, word or deed, as the chairman of the committee, the Speaker of the House of Representatives, or the President of the United States."

Mr. Upshaw then introduced Colonel Simmons to the committee. Colonel Simmons' testimony required several sessions, and he explained everything about the Ku Klux Klan from the time that he had founded the organization until the time of the hearing. Nothing in his testimony, and he was thoroughly cross-questioned by members of the committee, brought out any fact concerning the Klan which could be construed as damaging to that organization. The organization and operation of the "Invisible Empire" were gone into by Colonel Simmons in the minutest detail, and he filed with the committee a complete financial statement of the Klan, and copies of all its rituals, documents, records, and papers.

Colonel Simmons asked Chairman Campbell that his testimony be taken under oath, but that was declined.

The Imperial Wizard declared that the fight conducted against the Klan was similar to the attacks years ago on the Masons; as the same charges were made against them and the same effort to destroy them was made as had been made against the Knights of the Ku Klux Klan, this fight on the Masons resulting in the formation of a political anti-Masonic party at that time.

He denounced the World and declared if that paper, which was then the chief Democratic organ in New York, could succeed in forcing a Republican Congress to destroy a great American fraternal organization, it would react against the Republicans in the next elections, as the Ku Klux Klan, "with its hundreds of thousands of friends at the polls three years hence, would forget party lines and vote the Democratic ticket."

He declared that the Hearst papers had attacked the Klan purely from the desire to obtain more circulation.

Colonel Simmons created a very favorable impression on the committee, and he repeatedly declared in his testimony that the Klan courted the fullest investigation, and that he and his assistants desired the Rules Committee to report a resolution providing for a special congressional investigation, that nothing had been developed in corroboration of the charges of the World and the Hearst papers except one fact—that the Klan had collected large sums of money and distributed the same as all other large fraternal organizations do. The whole testimony did not develop any evidence where the Klan as a Klan had perpetrated any of the outrages charged against it in some of the Southern States.

The last day of the hearing, when Colonel Simmons had completed his testimony, the Associated Press story began with the following sentence: "The Ku Klux Klan investigation blew up today."

It was plain to unprejudiced observers that the investigation conducted by the House Rules Committee had resulted in a vindication of the Ku Klux Klan, and a repudiation of the charges made by the New York World and the Hearst papers. In fact, the World and Hearst attacks on the Klan really resulted in nothing, except giving the Klan a nation-wide publicity which was extraordinarily valuable to it in getting its name and principles before the American public, and an advertising which could not have been purchased for many millions of dollars. The Klan greatly profited by the newspaper attacks on it and the congressional investigation because as a result of these attacks and the investigation, for a long time afterwards it received daily thousands of applications for membership from all sections of the United States, and it seemed probable then that within a short time it would number more than one million members, all sworn to loyalty to the Flag, the Constitution, the Republic, and advocating Americanism, patriotism, and Anglo-Saxon supremacy.

CHAPTER XVIII

REORGANIZATION OF THE KLAN

The Washington investigation of the Klan in 1921 under the Simmons regime caused considerable dissatisfaction among Klan leaders in the various States, and at this time the Klan was organized in nearly all the States and the District of Columbia, in some of the States having a very large membership and great political influence. This was particularly so in New York, Indiana, and Ohio, and of course in practically all of the Southern States.

Some of the State leaders headed a movement to reorganize the Klan, and there was considerable sentiment among the rank and file that Imperial Wizard Simmons should retire from the chieftainship of the order.

The principal factor in this revolt was Dr. Hiram Wesley Evans, a dentist of Dallas, Texas. Dr. Evans was a Klan chieftain in Texas, and one of the most prominent and active of the State leaders of the organization.

The revolt was soon brought to a head led by Evans, but when Simmons was requested to retire it developed that he personally owned the copyright on everything that the Klan used that could be copyrighted — name,

DR. HIRAM WESLEY EVANS
Third Imperial Wizard — Knights of the Ku Klux Klan

140-a

ritual, constitution, charter, and everything else of any value in the organization.

The fact was that Simmons and E. Y. Clark were then practically the personal owners of the Klan, its name, property, and everything else that it possessed of value. Under the Simmons regime the Klan was run as sort of personal "racket" of Simmons and Clark, the rebels charged. They ostensibly had regular salaries but it is alleged they took what profits they pleased.

When the insurgent Klansmen sought to oust Simmons, they were up against the fact that Simmons and Clark practically owned the whole organization, except the membership.

So, in order to oust Simmons, Clark having left the organization for new fields some time previously, it was necessary to BUY SIMMONS OUT. This was done, Simmons being paid $140,000 cash for his copyrights on all the Klan material, after which Simmons "resigned", and Evans was elected Imperial Wizard, being installed head of the organization November 24, 1932.

It was reported that an unknown intermediary manipulated the "deal" whereby Simmons sold out his "holdings" in the Klan, and that the intermediary received from Simmons $40,000 "commission" for the sale.

Simmons took his profits and remained for some years in Atlanta, making several abortive efforts to organize similar organizations to the Klan, all of which ended in failure. He finally left Atlanta and is now living in retirement in Luverne, Alabama.

Under Evans the Klan, largely because of the Washington investigation, the retirement of Simmons and Clark, and particularly the business depression, began to rapidly lose membership and in a few years, when Evans was succeeded by Imperial Wizard James A. Colscott on June 12, 1939, the membership had gradually decreased from about 1,000,000 in its heyday during the Simmons management, to a few thousand.

When Evans secured control the Klan owned a large printing plant and a regalia factory in Buckhead, Georgia, (suburb of Atlanta), the "Imperial Palace" or headquarters in Atlanta, and an interest in other property in Atlanta, including Lanier University, which by the way was a university in name only, it never having been opened as an institution of learning by the Klan.

Loss of membership and consequent loss of revenue caused the Klan to gradually go down hill as an organization, but in some States, particularly in its birth-State, Georgia, it still was a powerful secret society. A very large number of prominent Georgians and public officials are still members. This is so in Alabama and Florida. Former U.S. Senator Hugo Black, of Alabama, was once a member and is now an Associate Justice of the U. S. Supreme Court.

During the Evans administration the "Imperial Palace" was sold to the Catholic Church, the printing plant was disposed of, and the regalia factory was sold. Other property of the Klan was otherwise disposed of, so that the only property remaining is the headquarters in Buckhead (1940), a large office building, that for a time was used as an apartment house.

When Evans obtained control he made one very important reform. All officials connected with headquarters were paid regular and reasonable salaries, instead of as under the Simmons management when Simmons and his associates looked on the organization as their private property, and for a time, at least, paid themselves large sums out of the receipts from membership and sale of regalia, it was alleged.

Evans strove mightily for almost 17 years to build up the Klan but conditions were against him, particularly business depression during the Roosevelt presidency, which was worse in the South where the Klan was strongest, than in the North.

Another reform instituted by Evans was a complete reversal of the original Simmons policy of the Klan's hostility to Catholics. Little was said about negroes or Jews during his time but Evans became very friendly with leading Catholics, on one occasion being guest at a dinner in Atlanta of very prominent Catholic prelates.

Evans, during all his administration, strongly advocated patriotism and Americanism, and many times condemned Communism and other "isms" that were soon after he became Imperial Wizard, beginning to rear their ugly heads in the United States.

One of Dr. Evans' statements regarding Communism, appeared soon after he became Imperial Wizard, in the Kourier, one of the then official publications of the Klan, as follows:

"COMMUNISM RAMPANT," by Dr. Hiram Wesley Evans, Imperial Wizard.

"Communism is a product of Bolshevism. It does not believe in private property, but that everything belongs to all. It does not believe in an organized government, but in anarchy. Communism does not believe in homes, but in sex nests. It terminates Motherhood and Fatherhood at birth. It not only does not believe in a personal God, or in any God, but is fighting God. Communism is exactly opposed to everything that Americans hold sacred. Hence, we in the Klan are unalterably opposed to Communism.

"The growth of Communism in the United States has caused many of our leading citizens to become pessimistic as to the future of our form of Government.

"We in the Klan are opposed to all who seek to change our form of Government. We are in favor of the Constitution of the United States of America, of Presidents and Congresses, of Judges and Juries and that in the form established by the founders of this Republic. We know that our form of Government has not failed, but on the other hand no other country has ever provided for its citizens as great an opportunity for the pursuit of happiness, for internal peace and security, and for economic prosperity as has the United States of America.

"We know that Communism is against God because the Government of Russia has legislated against God. We in the Klan cannot imagine a country to be successful and prosperous whose citizens do not love, revere and obey God.

"The Klan knows that: Marriage is a sacret institution — that the responsibilities of parents last throughout their lives — that homes are the finest achievement of our civilization — and that American homes are the finest homes in all the world.

"Nowadays, wherever civil life begins, groups of paid agitators appear, fomenting disorder and preaching rebellion. While they claim to be working in the interests of the people, we know that it is not in the interests of the people for our Government to be destroyed and for Anarchy or Absolutism to take its place. It is against reason, for God to be displaced in our social and spiritual life; for our homes to be only nesting places cannot possibly be in the interests of our people. All these things will come to pass if Communists are permitted to have their way. Of course they are not going to have their way. Our people are too sane to become converts to any such noxious, unstable and illusory theory.

How Shall We Fight?

"There are millions who have solemnly sworn to defend and protect our Constitution and Government. The time has come for them to fulfill their sacred promises. We know that they believe in Americanism rather than Bolshevism, but it is not enough for them to believe in Americanism, they must do something about it. Strong men must stand up and be counted.

"We prepared the Klan for the hour that is now here. While the maintenance of our Organization is IMPORTANT, unselfish service to God and Country is ALL IMPORTANT. We shall seek and find those who have sworn to serve, and shoulder to shoulder we will ride to

145

defend constituted authority against civil strife and rebellion.

"There are many millions who have never joined the Klan who believe in the same noble principles which we so earnestly espouse. We shall send every Klansman who took the oath at our altars as evangels to find all those upon whom our country can depend.

"The President of our land, with the other officials of the law, are our rulers. We owe them obedience and support against civil strife. We are now preparing to be a bulwark of strength to them in every important place throughout the land. It is a great opportunity for us to do signal service. A united Klan, wholly unselfish in its purpose, can restore confidence in our form of Government and will PREVENT CIVIL STRIFE throughout the land."

This statement and similar Klan publicity drew attention of the Communists and Fascists to the Klan, and efforts were made to buy the organization, all of which were vigourously repelled by Evans.

Henry D. Allen, one-time Silver Shirt leader, and a secret agent of the mysterious Mrs. Leslie Fry, alias Paquita Louise De Shishmareff, testified before the Dies committee that Mrs. Fry sent him to Atlanta to buy the Klan, and Fry offered Dr. Evans $75,000 for the Klan. Allen testified that "Evans was not interested in the idea."

The mysterious Mrs. Fry, when sought by the committee for questioning, could not be located, and is believed to have fled the United States. This woman was once leader of the alleged "Militant Christian Patriots," thought to be secretly backed by White Russian organizations and Italian Fascists. At any rate the Klan was not and is not for sale.

JAMES A. COLESCOTT
Imperial Wizard in his official robes as supreme head of the Klan

148

CHAPTER XIX

. A NEW IMPERIAL WIZARD TAKES CHARGE

Dr. Evans, after years of struggling with Klan problems, decided to retire as Imperial Wizard, which he did on June 12, 1939, being succeeded by James A. Colescott, who had for some time been his principal assistant in the Atlanta headquarters, and who had been connected with the Klan in various capacities for many years. Mr. Colescott was unanimously elected Imperial Wizard by 36 State Klan heads on that date in Atlanta, and has since been actively in charge of all Klan affairs.

Though in complete charge of the Klan for little more than two years at this writing, Imperial Wizard Colescott has infused an immense amount of new life in the organization, and the membership is again increasing at a rapid rate. Since his election Colescott has visited practically every State in the Union, conferring with Klan leaders in each State, and stimulating a renewed interest in the old and new Klan members. His headquarters is in the old Buckhead (Atlanta suburb) office building, where he is assisted by a large staff of vigorous and competent assistants.

The total membership of the Klan is always kept

secret, but it was learned that the new Imperial Wizard anticipates an increase in membership in the next twelve months of more than 200,000 members. It is believed the Klan membership is now close to 500,000.

Colescott has had long experience in Klan work, having come up from the ranks in the Klan, so to speak, and is a man of great executive ability and tremendous energy. He has the complete confidence of the officers and membership of the Klan, and as he is comparatively a young man and devotes all his time day and night to the affairs of the Knights, it would seem that the organization under his management may again reach in time well into the millions of members that it once had.

Not the least of the work of the New Imperial Wizard, which leads an observer to believe that the Klan is rapidly "coming back," is the policy of toleration instituted by Colescott, and his stern disapproval of any local Klan starting crusades against Catholics, Jews or negroes.

The following appeared in the *Florida Times-Union*, of Jacksonville, Florida, under a Miami date of November 20, 1939, which well illustrates the policies of the new Imperial Wizard:

"Klan's Methods of Intimidation are Abandoned"

"New Imperial Wizard Says He Will Not Tolerate Such Practices"

Miami, Nov. 20. — J. A. Colescott, of Atlanta, new imperial wizard of the Ku Klux Klan, said today he did not "intend to tolerate" such methods of intimidation as the burning of fiery crosses and parades of white-robed figures through negro sections that occurred before a city election here last fall.

"There are more intelligent American ways to handle such problems," Colescott said. "I would rather see the Klan disorganized than see it continue its old policy of anti-Semitism, anti-Catholicism or anti-alienism."

The imperial wizard, here to complete a State-wide Klan reorganization, said he was accused "of selling out to the Jews" by some Klansmen at the convocation in Atlanta last June.

"Jews have equal rights under the Constitution," he declared, "and as far as the Klan is concerned, they are entitled to those rights. We have not compromised the basic creed of the Klan, however. We have not added to or taken away any of our aims, for the Klan always will be devoted to preservation of patriotism."

The Klan would not be an organization, he said, directed against the Jews or any other minority groups.

"There has been a lot of controversy in this State because of certain former Klan leaders' anti-Semitic attitude and misdirected efforts," he declared, "and I intend to see the Klan completely reorganized here, as in other States, on a sound basis of Americanism. Within the last two months some 25 Klan leaders in Florida, including eight in Miami, have been relieved of their commands for that reason."

Nothing could better illustrate the plans and policies of Colescott, and it is believed that this policy will do more than anything else to assist in again building up the Klan membership.

On December 5, 1939 the following appeared in the Detroit, Michigan, *Evening Times*:

IMPERIAL WIZARD HERE TO REVIVE KU KLUX KLAN

THE FIERY CROSS—SYMBOL OF THE KU KLUX KLAN—

WILL BLAZE AGAIN IN DETROIT

This was revealed today by James A. Colescott, imperial wizard, who is in Detroit to complete plans to reorganize the Klan in this area and throughout the state. Pointing out that no fundamental changes have been made in the Klan, Colescott outlined a program which will include combating all "isms" and opposition to radical leadership in labor unions.

"We do not feel that there is any place in American life for any ism of foreign origin," he said. "We hope to destroy them through exposing them for what they are.

"As for radical leadership in labor organizations, we have advised our people to affiliate themselves with unions with a view toward electing union officials capable of recognizing American principles."

Colescott, who is no stranger to Detroit, having headed the local Klan organization during its heyday in 1924, declined to reveal the organization's membership in Detroit but declared a 22 per cent increase has been noted since last June. In 1924, the Klan had a local membership of 32,000 persons, Colescott said. At that time, adverse publicity and the ensuing depression all but wrecked the organization.

Colescott said:

"I have begun already weeding out irresponsible groups

in the organization. One of the things that will not be tolerated any more is Klan intimidations or the forceful breaking up of any group which we oppose."

Under the reorganization plans, the Klan will discard the mask, leaving only the gown and cap as its official regalia. This outfit will be sold to members by the home office for $3.50, bringing a profit of 90 cents. The sale of official robes to members ($6.50) at an exorbitant price was one of the things under Simmons that caused criticism.

This excerpt also tells something of the new policies of the Klan, and will go a long way toward allaying any mistaken hostility that may still exist against it.

Imperial Wizard Colescott is 43 years old, a native of Terre Haute, Ind., born there January 11, 1897. He was educated in the Terre Haute public schools, and graduated at the Terre Haute Veterinary College in 1917. Almost immediately he enlisted in the U.S. Regular Army, served 22 months in France in the World War, taking part in five major offensives, and was with the American Army of Occupation in Germany. In 1918 he was commissioned a lieutenant in the Remount Service, and was honorably mustered out in 1921. He then practiced his profession in Terre Haute, but in 1922 became connected with the Klan, which then had a very large membership and an immense political influence in Indiana. He has therefore been continuously connected with the Klan for approximately 18 years, in various capacities, and probably because of this long service knows more about the organization than any other high officer of the K.K.K. His service included office in Indiana, and for nearly nine years he was Grand Dragon or State head of the Klan in Ohio, with headquarters in Columbus during which time the Ohio membership was over 200,000. He has been Grand Dragon for eight mid-Western States.

Colescott is a handsome, very intelligent and attractive man of medium size, and shows in his manner and bearing his military service. He is a Master Mason, an Odd Fellow, and a member of the American Legion. He is happily married and the father of a 14-year-old daughter. His home is in Atlanta, but he is rarely there, spending nearly all his time traveling over the country building up the Klan.

Colescott has instituted a real business system in the Atlanta Klan headquarters, and the society's affairs are conducted with accuracy and dispatch. There is no "racket," no "graft," no "rake-offs" in his management. Annual dues of Klansmen are now $6 per year, of which 90 cents is sent to Atlanta Headquarters. This is quite different, when under the Simmons "ownership" at least one-fourth of all the $10 initiation dues, as well as annual membership dues, went into Klan headquarters.

Colescott said in Atlanta recently:

"The future of this Republic rests solely in the hands of native-born, white, Protestant, gentile citizens. This does not mean that Catholics, Jews, negroes and foreigners cannot vote or be elected to office, or take part in civic affairs."

Colescott doesn't hate negroes. He even has a negro maid to take care of his daughter when he is away organizing the Klan. He even paid this maid's wages and medical bills when she was sick recently.

"Among my friends," he said recently, "are Roman Catholics and Jews. There is no reason why Americans cannot get along together."

Colescott declared there are 6,000,000 aliens in the United States holding jobs while 10,000,000 native Americans are out of work.

Recently in an open telegram to Representative Martin Dies, chairman of the House Committee on Un-American Activities, Colescott said:

"Every true American, and that includes every Klansman, is behind you and your committee in its effort to turn the country back to the honest, freedom-loving, God-fearing American to whom it belongs."

Colescott laid particular emphasis on "men and women, many of them high in the councils of the Administration, who quietly work for the cause of communism."

In a recent press interview Colescott called on all Klansmen in the nation to oppose America's becoming involved in the European war.

"The bloody quarrels of the Old War are no concern of ours," he said. "All we gained from the first World War was a united hatred of America, plus a mad-dog reign of dictators, fuehrers, and prime ministers."

No real American can quarrel with the sentiments and public utterances of Colescott since he became Im-

155

perial Wizard. Under his guidance the Klan is evidently headed for a great success, for its principles are sound Americanism and loyal patriotism to our Flag.

Colescott has recently revived publication of the *Fiery Cross*, official Klan newspaper, which circulates throughout the country.

Any native-born patriotic American who investigates the present purposes of the Klan and the policies of Colescott, as repeatedly announced, cannot help but be favorably inclined to the reviving K.K.K.

It now seems destined to become the greatest of all American secret societies.

CHAPTER XX

THE SYMBOL AND THE SLOGAN
OF THE KLAN

The symbol of a well-known life insurance company is that famous rock which towers above the entrance of the Mediterranean Sea. Fortified by Great Britain, it commands the gates to the Atlantic, and helps to make England mistress of the seas. "Impregnable as Gibraltar" is a slogan denoting faith in self and uttering defiance to all efforts, however gigantic, to put down the defenses of a man or the fortifications of an institution.

In Georgia, the Imperial State of the South, where the Ku Klux Klan was reborn, we have a rock which will become as famous to American patriots as Gibraltar. Rising from an almost level plain, as if brooking no precipitous rival, defying the storms of centuries, stands "Stone Mountain," near Atlanta. It is a solid block of gray granite, seventeen hundred and eighty feet high, several miles in circumference at its base, sloping on one side, precipitous on the other. On the sheer front of the precipice a famous sculptor,[1] inspired by patriotic women of the South, carved out of the rock, running for hundreds of feet along its face, heroic scenes, figures and battles of the war between the States.[2] On this gigantic canvas of imperishable granite we shall see the Blue and the Gray contending in the mighty shock of battle at Chancellorsville and Atlanta, Chickamauga and Gettysburg; we shall see their leaders — Grant and Lee, Gordon and Sheridan, and many others of lesser fame, and Lincoln the Great, and Davis, leader of the ill-starred Confederacy; and Appomattox where the fratricidal strife ended, and the Stars and Bars was folded in undying memories, and the Stars and Stripes became once more the unsullied flag of a reunited nation, "one and inseparable, now and forever."

These sculptures on Stone Mountain will be the greatest in the world — greater than the Sphinx whose stony lips have kept silence for centuries along the banks of the Nile, where the Pharaohs forced their helpless subjects to build marvels of architecture, where the lotus bloomed in langorous beauty, and where one or more of the Wise Men, guided by the marvelous Star, rode to find and worship the world's Redeemer lying a helpless babe in the manger at Bethlehem. These pictured battles and charging warriors on the precipice of Stone Mountain will become more famous than the Lion of Lucerne carved by Thorwaldsen on the face of an Alpine cliff as a memorial to the Swiss Guard who fell in the line of duty.

---

[1] Gutson Borglum.

[2] The work has not been finished. A new commission of prominent men is now being organized to complete it.

Only sixteen miles from Atlanta, Stone Mountain, because of its solitary and majestic grandeur, will become more and more an object of national if not international interest. Not only geologists and other scientists will visit this granite monolith, but also artists and other lovers of scenic beauty and majesty. Not only those of the South will come, but also thousands of tourists from colder regions and foreign lands will visit the homes and haunts of Dixie and learn of the traditions, the chivalry, and the abounding hospitality of the South.

Why has the Ku Klux Klan chosen Stone Mountain as its symbol? Because its beauty, its majesty, its impregnability typified the character, the purposes and the perpetuity of the order. What better place could be found for the reincarnation of the Ku Klux Klan than this giant granite monument of Nature? To its summit, during a stormy night in 1915, while blustering winds blew, Col. William J. Simmons, who had caught the vision of the great Order, led thirty-four leading citizens of Atlanta. They were ministers, lawyers, physicians, judges, merchants, teachers, laborers — a democratic assembly where all were equal. These thirty-four men were to constitute the solid nucleus around whom should gather good and true men from every quarter of America, men who, like Sir Philip Sidney, were cavaliers without fear and without reproach. The fiery cross blazed as a gonfalon, striking with wonder the inhabitants of the villages clustered about the base of the mountain. Its gleaming arms scintillated as if they were the resounding voice of a reborn Stentor announcing to all the world faith in American institutions, and the hope that white supremacy and true liberty should prevail from the stormy Atlantic to the golden shores of California lapped by the rolling Pacific; from New England's rockbound coast to the orange flowers and magnolia blooms of the land where Ponce de Leon sought the fountain of perpetual youth; from the Great Lakes separating us from our peaceful neighbor, Canada, to the illimitable plains of Texas and the Rio Grande bordering the land of the Montezumas and the Aztecs shrouded in the mists of history.

Colonel Simmons, the valiant leader of that band of forward-looking patriots, lifted his tall form on the highest peak of the mountain. The air seemed vibrant with voices out of the heroic past, telling of the deeds of the fathers, uttering encouragement for the present, making prognostications for the future. In earnest and heart-compelling words Colonel Simmons told his thirty-four listeners that he had been called to the work of reviving the Ku Klux Klan, and had not been disobedient to the vision. He said that the Klan must be made a fraternal order larger and grander than its prototype, destined, as he hoped, to spread throughout the country until it had members in every state and section. No one should be allowed to become a Klansman unless his character was good, his motives altruistic, his purposes lofty, his honor pledged to law and order, to one hundred per cent Americanism, to nation-wide and, finally, world-wide supremacy of the Anglo-Saxon race. He asserted his apprehension that an inevitable conflict between the white race on the one side and the yellow and black races on the other was indicated by the present international unrest. This conflict would be Armageddon, unless the Anglo-Saxon, in unity with the Latin and Teutonic nations, should take the leadership of the world and show to all that it had and would hold the world mastery forever.

Colonel Simmons then gave to the thirty-four present the opportunity of becoming charter members of the new movement. In the war for Texan independence, the Alamo at San Antonio, with less than two hundred defenders, was besieged by Santa Ana leading an army of four thousand Mexicans. Colonel Travis mustered his men in the court of the old stone church, turned into a fort, and told them that, if they closed the gates before the siege began, all would die; but before the gates were closed, there was a chance to escape, and anyone might take that chance without shame, as life was dear to all. Then, drawing a line on the floor with the point of his sword, Travis said: "Each must decide for himself. Let him who is willing to die for Texas independence, cross over the line!" Every man crossed, and every man died, but Texas was free! On the monument erected to their valor in the Capitol park at Austin, is the sentence: "Thermopylae had her messenger of defeat; the Alama had none!" The heroism of Travis and his men was repaid when General Houston swept Santa Ana and his army to destruction at the battle of San Jacinto.

So, every one who heard Colonel Simmons' call to patriotic service in a time of peace, knelt on the rocky slope of Stone Mountain, under the silent, solemn stars,

161

and took the oath of consecration to the ideals, purposes and work of the Ku Klux Klan.

From this start, awe-inspiring yet humble, the Ku Klux Klan has had a phenomenal growth. It has been fought from without and within; investigated by a Congressional committee and by judicial action; charged with crimes and misdemeanors by wicked men who claimed membership to cover their nefarious deeds; its leading officials traduced and slandered. Yet it has maintained a loyal, successful and enthusiastic organization to this day.

What of its future? This is most promising. A storm may be unpleasant and even terrifying, but it clears the atmosphere. A lightning bolt may shake the earth, but its fierce flame consumes nephitic vapors that might cause contagion and death. So, when the Ku Klux Klan has beaten down all attacks from without; when it has purged itself from disloyal traitors from within; then, like a giant refreshed by sleep, it will gird itself for the struggle and run with patience and increasing success its appointed race.

The Anglo-Saxon is the typeman of history. To him must yield the self-centered Hebrew, the cultured Greek, the virile Roman, the mystic Oriental. The psalmist must have had him in mind by poetic imagination when he struck his sounding harp and sang: "O Lord: thou hast made him a little lower than the angels, and hast crowned him with glory and honor. Thou madest him to have dominion over the works of thy hands; thou hast put all things under his feet." The Ku Klux Klan desires that its ruling members shall be of this all-conquering blood.

162

This does not mean prohibition against other white bloods. The Constitution of the United States ordains that no man shall be President of this great Republic unless he was born in America. This is no reflection on Lloyd George, or Poincare, or Albert of Belgium. It is simply the preference and mandate of our republic. A man may come to America from other lands who may be a greater man than the President; but we have decided, and we have the right to decide, that our President shall be American born. So, the Ku Klux Klan was planned for the white American. But, as the United States welcomes to its hospitable shores all who will become Americans by loyal adoption and by swearing allegiance to the Constitution, so the Ku Klux Klan welcomes into membership any and all who are white Americans, speaking one language, glad to live under the aegis of the Constitution, and thrilled when they see the Stars and Stripes wave its brilliant folds in the breezes of freedom that fan the cheeks of all true patriots irrespective of former nationality or political condition.

In brief, the Ku Klux Klan desires to be, hopes to be, plans to be and will be a great, influential, helpful, patriotic, American fraternal order, taking its allotted place with similar secret brotherhoods, and with them working out our Christian civilization, adding to the gifts and graces, the prosperity and happiness of mankind, and standing for the noble, the true and the good, for the majesty of law, for the advancement of the human race.

CHAPTER XXI

KU KLUX KLAN AIDS ROOSEVELT

President Franklin D. Roosevelt is one of the smartest (if not the smartest) politicians that ever attained the Presidency of the United States. He has always been an opportunist. His first move to obtain the Presidential nomination of the Democratic Party was when as governor of New York he established the Warms Springs, Georgia, sanitarium for infantile paralysis patients, and let it be known far and wide he had made 'Georgia his other home.' This was a cunning maneuver to obtain the support of the South for his presidential ambitions, for 'his other home' in Georgia where he owns a farm at Warm Springs and dominates the infantile paralysis Foundation, is in the heart of the South, and the South at that time, before, after he became President and caused to be abolished the two-thirds rule in national Democratic Conventions, very largely dictated or at least agreed to the presidential nominees of the Party. Once President and in control of the Party, his abolition of the two-thirds rule for presidential nominations took away the immense political power before wielded by the South in national Democratic conventions. Having ridden into the White House with the help of the

South and its two-thirds rule, he took care to take away that power from the very section that was largely responsible for his first nomination for the Presidency at Chicago.

In all his career Mr. Roosevelt has not hesitated to use every kind and any kind of support available for his advancement.

He largely secured the support of the South with the fiction of 'Georgia my other home' and the public sympathy for the infantile paralysis so-called charity. It should be noted that patients at Warm Springs Foundation pay weekly rates the same as at any other sanitarium for the treatment of various maladies. There is little 'charity' about it. It is run for profit.

But where he made his greatest play for the Southern delegates for his first nomination was thru the Roosevelt Southern Clubs (organized in 1930 in Atlanta), which was partially dominated by the celebrated Ku Klux Klan, at that time headed by Dr. Hiram W. Evans, Imperial Wizard, who had succeeded to the Chieftainship of the Klan by the retirement of Col. William J. Simmons, the founder of the modern Klan.

The Roosevelt Southern Clubs was organized on Christmas Day, 1930, and in a career of about 18 months, with headquarters in the Kimball House in Atlanta, organized Democratic leaders in 17 Southern, Southeastern, and Southwest States, forming 17 State organizations for Roosevelt's nomination (at that time he was serving his second term as governor of New York) with managers in each State, and organizing more than 1,000 Roosevelt-for-President Clubs in those States. This organization, coupled with the "Georgia my other home" fallacy and the national sympathy caused by the Warm Springs infantile paralysis alleged charity, plus the Ku Klux Klan influence, secured all the States mentioned for Mr. Roosevelt's first nomination for the Presidency.

The campaign of the Roosevelt-for-President Clubs was launched and carried on about a year BEFORE usual pre-nomination campaigns, and the South "was in the bag," to use one of Jim Farley's favorite expressions, before other candidates for the Presidency knew what it was all about.

After the South had been secured for Roosevelt other candidates for the Presidency woke up to what had occurred and made belated and futile efforts to line up Southern delegates, notably in the case of the late Newton D. Baker, of Cleveland, Ohio, Secretary of War in President Wilson's World War Cabinet, who was an active candidate. Mr. Baker's emissaries visited the South about a year before the 1932 Chicago Convention and after a survey of conditions and learning what the Roosevelt-for-President Clubs had accomplished ,abandoned their hunt for delegates in that section, and left the Southern field to the astute Mr. Roosevelt. The Roosevelt-for-President Clubs were organized in Atlanta, and working thru the South a long time before Roosevelt appointed Jim Farley as his campaign manager.

The general chairman of the Roosevelt Southern Clubs, after it got well under way in the Kimball House headquarters in Atlanta, was Judge Paul S. Etheridge, of Atlanta. Mr. Etheridge for a long time was general counsel for the Klan under the Simmons regime, has served as one of Fulton County's (Atlanta) five commissioners, and is now a superior court Judge of Fulton County. He is a prominent churchman and was one of the best known and esteemed lawyers in Georgia before his elevation to the Superior Court bench.

Following was the organization of the Roosevelt Southern Clubs, copied from one of the Clubs' first letterheads:

DR. LUTHER P. BAKER, HONORARY CHAIRMAN
F. B. SUMMERS, EXECUTIVE CHAIRMAN
A. O. KEMPER, SECRETARY
C. W. JONES, TREASURER

VICE CHAIRMAN AT LARGE
R. K. DANIEL

VICE CHAIRMEN FOR STATES
WARREN S. REESE, JR., FOR ALABAMA
E. G. WILLIAMS, FOR MISSISSIPPI
ARTHUR RHORER, FOR KENTUCKY
CLAUD N. SAPP, FOR SOUTH CAROLINA
J. WALLACE WINBORNE, FOR NORTH CAROLINA
THOMAS A. EDWARDS, FOR LOUISIANA

ROOSEVELT SOUTHERN CLUBS

A South-Wide Volunteer Organization Advocating the Nomination and Election of Governor Franklin D. Roosevelt, of New York, as President of the United States. Organized December 25, 1930.

SUITE 510 KIMBALL HOUSE
TELEPHONE JACKSON 7700
ATLANTA, GA.

Leaders of the Ku Klux Klan, from the first inception of the Roosevelt candidacy for the Presidency, were enthusiastic for the Roosevelt nomination.

At that time they did not know that Jim Farley, a devout Catholic, who has within the past kissed Pope Pius' 12th toe in fealty at the Vatican, received the Pope's blessing and medals for himself and members of his family who accompanied the Postmaster General on his pilgrimages to Rome, was to be the main wheelhorse in the Roosevelt campaign for the nomination for the Presidency.

It was a great combination: The Ku Klux in the South and the Catholics in New England and the North. This was playing both ends against the middle, but Mr. Roosevelt always knew how to take the fullest advantage of circumstances and conditions. He is not only an opportunist but a great realist.

This combination of Catholics and Ku Klux was carefully kept from the public, there was no comment on it in newspapers, and few except the "inside camarilla" around Roosevelt knew of the strange political bed fellows. At that time the Klan had made no effort to suppress its original prejudice against Jews, Catholics and Negroes. That came later just as the regime of Imperial Wizard Evans was drawing to a close in 1939.

168

The alliance of the Ku Kluxers and the Knights of Columbus effected, the super-politician Roosevelt, guided by the master intriguer Farley, began to pull wires and effect political combinations that eventually dragged the Negro vote away from the Republican Party, and practically incorporated the "black belts" thru the country in the Democratic ranks.

The following correspondence illumines the part played by the Klan in the Roosevelt pre-nomination campaign in the South.

Part of the work of the Roosevelt Southern Clubs included efforts to interest powerful fraternal and secret organizations for Governor Roosevelt's cause.

Among others, high officials of the Ku Klux Klan were interested early in the campaign. The Ku Klux Klan officials favored, at that time, Governor Roosevelt's nomination, and supplied the office furniture for the headquarters of the Roosevelt Southern Clubs in the Kimball House in Atlanta, the work of the Clubs having grown so by this time that it was necessary to move out of an office building into larger headquarters in a hotel where visitors and politicians could be conferred with. Politicians began to visit the headquarters from many sections of the South.

The Ku Klux Klan furniture which equipped the headquarters of the Roosevelt Southern Clubs in the Kimball House was secured through the following correspondence:

On Christmas Day, 1930, the following telegram was sent to Governor Roosevelt:

169

December 25, 1930

Governor Franklin D. Roosevelt,
Albany, N.Y.

Please permit us to tender you today the South's Christmas Present in the form of organization here today of the "Roosevelt Southern Clubs," planned to include formation throughout all the Southern States of Roosevelt-for-President Clubs, and the establishment of an active Southern press bureau to advocate your nomination and election as President of the United States. The "Roosevelt Southern Clubs" plans to act as a center and clearing house for Roosevelt-for-President Clubs in the entire South. We salute you as the next occupant of the White House, and send Merry Christmas and a Happy New Year.

F. B. SUMMERS
Acting Chairman, Roosevelt Southern Clubs

Dear Mr. Spratt:

January 13, 1931
CONFIDENTIAL

American Printing & Manufacturing Co.,
Ku Klux Klan Building, Buckhead, Atlanta, Ga.
Attention Mr. H. C. Spratt, Secretary

In regard to conversations with Doctor Evans and your kind offer, with his approval, to loan the Roosevelt Southern Clubs office furniture for the Clubs' headquarters, we thank you. We could use 4 flat top desks and one typewriter desk for the present.

We are obliged to you for offering to aid the movement to make Governor Roosevelt President of the United States. No doubt the Ku Klux Klan influence, which we understand from Doctor Evans and yourself, is favorable to Governor Roosevelt, will be of immense assistance not only in the South and Southwest where we will operate, but all over the United States. We thank you for the furniture and offers of yourself and Doctor Evans to cooperate, and certainly appreciate it highly.

Of course this transaction must be kept absolutely secret, for obvious reasons. Should it become known that the Klan is supporting the Governor it might prove very damaging with the Catholic and Jewish vote, and with other classes that oppose your organization.

Sincerely yours,

ROOSEVELT SOUTHERN CLUBS

Per F. L. Eyles, Jr., Acting Vice Chairman

(Dr. Evans was then the Imperial Wizard of the Klan).

The Klan replied:

IMPERIAL PALACE

INVISIBLE EMPIRE

KNIGHTS OF THE KU KLUX KLAN

Atlanta, Georgia

January 14, 1931

Roosevelt Southern Clubs,
226 Terminal Building,
Atlanta, Ga.

Gentlemen:—

We are today delivering to ZABAN STORAGE COMPANY five desks as follows:

1 flat top desk 35½ inches by 60 inches
1 flat top desk 37½ inches by 72 inches
1 flat top desk 24 inches by 60 inches
1 flat top desk 34 inches by 60 inches
1 typewriter desk

This action is taken in accordance with your letter of January 13, 1931.

Sincerely yours,

AMERICAN PRINTING & MANUFACTURING CO.

(Klan Printing Plant)

ROOSEVELT SOUTHERN CLUBS

(Temporary Organization)

226-27 Terminal Building

Telephone Walnut 9397

Atlanta, Ga.

February 2, 1931

Mr. H. C. Spratt, Manager
American Printing & Mfg. Co.,
P. O. Box 1204
Atlanta, Georgia.
Dear Mr. Spratt:

Referring to our conversation of January 31, we would like very much to borrow the furniture you mentioned, which consists of one table, one desk, and one swivel chair.

The furniture will be used in our headquarters in the Kimball House, where it will be subject to your call. We will keep it in good condition and will be greatly indebted if you will let us use this furniture.

Yours truly,

F. L. EYLES, JR.

Advocating the Nomination and Election of Governor Franklin D. Roosevelt, of New York, for President.

This was additional furniture to the first shipment. The Klan loaned about half of the entire office equipment of the Club's headquarters.

The Klan hastened to comply with this request:

AMERICAN PRINTING & MANUFACTURING COMPANY

The Roosevelt Southern Clubs,
Kimball House,
Atlanta, Georgia.

Gentlemen:

We have your request for some additional furniture to be used in your Southern Headquarters.

We have today delivered to Zaban Storage Company, one flat-top desk, one swivel chair and one two-drawer table. All of the above articles are mahogany.

We are pleased to accommodate you in this matter.

Very truly yours,

AMERICAN PRINTING & MANUFACTURING CO.

(No date on this letter, but it was in January, 1931).

Hon. Paul S. Etheridge, mentioned above, who was then chairman of the Fulton County Commission, former general counsel for the Ku Klux Klan, then became general chairman of the Roosevelt Southern Clubs. Mr. Etheridge's connection with the Roosevelt Southern Clubs was a big advantage in the propaganda work for Governor Roosevelt throughout the entire South and Southwest, where the Ku Klux Klan was powerful politically and socially.

Mr. Etheridge gave out a number of press notices. The following is a sample:

"Governor Franklin D. Roosevelt, of New York, undoubtedly will capture the presidential nomination at the Chicago convention," declared Hon. Paul S. Etheridge, general chairman of the Roosevelt Southern Clubs and chairman of the Fulton County Commission, in a statement today.

"A careful analysis of the situation to date shows that Governor Roosevelt will enter the convention with somewhere around 650 or 700 votes. A number of the favorite sons, after the first ballot, will turn to Franklin D. Roosevelt, which assures his nomination on the second or third ballot.

It is a great satisfaction to the friends of Gov. Roosevelt that the movement to nominate him was inaugurated in Georgia, his other home."

After the Roosevelt Campaign in the South, Southeast and Southwest had ended with a complete victory for Roosevelt in this entire section, the Ku Klux Klan furniture was returned to the Klan, with exception of some that was shipped to Savannah, Ga., on order of the Klan.

Sept. 23, 1931

Hon. James A. Farley, Chairman,
Democratic State Committee,
331 Madison Avenue,
New York City.
Dear Mr. Farley:

I read your letter to Mr. Summers, of date of September 19. Mr. Summers would have written you today, but he has been indisposed and at home for a few days. We do not know when he can be in New York, but feel sure that when he does get there he will take great pleasure in conferring with you over the Roosevelt chances in the South and Southwest.

Our work is progressing at a great rate. I feel sure that we will succeed on a great scale with the effort being made to make Mr. Roosevelt President.

One of our friends who is a warm Roosevelt partisan (converted to the cause by ourselves) who is a high official in the Ku Klux Klan, will soon be in New York and I will give him a letter of introduction to you. This organization, though you may not know it, is secretly aiding us in many ways and the officials, or some of them, are very friendly to us personally and are our friends. I do not belong to the Klan myself, but have many friends who do, and I feel absolutely sure of their support.

Personally I hope to have the pleasure of soon talking over the situation in the South and Southwest with you. You can count absolutely on Georgia going solid for Roosevelt.

With regards,

Sincerely yours,

F. L. EYLES, JR.

175

DEMOCRATIC STATE COMMITTEE
331 Madison Avenue
New York City

Sept. 30, 1931

Mr. F. B. Summers,
Roosevelt Southern Clubs,
Suite 310, Kimball House,
Atlanta, Ga.
Dear Mr. Summers:

I received your very interesting letter of September 25th. In it you indicate that you are going to be in New York on October 12th. I do hope I will have the pleasure of seeing you and going over with you the conditions in the Southern States.

I read with interest copy of the letter you received from Senator Joseph E. Robinson of Kentucky. I think it would be a better plan if you gave out the result of that letter down in your city, rather than have it issued from this office, although we are glad to have the information.

I am sure that you will see Gvernor Roosevelt before you receive this letter and go over with him whatever you desire to discuss regarding the situation in your section of the country.

Anticipating the pleasure of seeing you soon, I am,
Sincerely yours,
JAMES A. FARLEY,

Because of differences over the State management in Alabama by the Roosevelt-for-President Clubs headquarters and Chairman Farley, and Roosevelt's and Farley's failure to keep promises both had made to reimburse the Clubs for about $7,400 it had advanced for expenses of the Atlantic headquarters and the Roosevelt pre-nomination campaign, Chairman Summers and Jones, who had by them organized the thousand or more clubs, sued Roosevelt on May 20, 1932, in the U. S. Court for the Northern district of Georgia. Excerpt of the bill follows:

Plaintiffs' actual expenditures in this behalf amounted to $7,400, of which sum there was contributed by parties other than defendant $860, leaving a balance of expenditures incurred and advanced by plaintiffs of $6,540, for which sum said defendant is liable to these plaintiffs by reason of the facts aforesaid.

WHEREFORE, plaintiffs pray for judgment for said sum, and that the regular process or subpoena of this Court issue and be served upon the defendant at the place where he is sojourning, which is within the jurisdiction of this court.

J. IRA HARRELSON,

STATE OF GEORGIA,
COUNTY OF FULTON.

Personally appeared F. B. SUMMERS and C. W. JONES, the plaintiffs in the above case, who being duly sworn deposes and says that the facts stated in the foregoing petition are true.

Sworn to and subscribed before me,

this the 20th day of May, 1932.

JEWELL BRYANT.

When Mr. Roosevelt was served on a train May 25, 1932, in Atlanta, with the suit in the Federal Court he gave out the following press statement:

"Many hundreds of people in every state in the union have done me the honor of organizing clubs and otherwise working in my behalf for many months past.

"These were wholly spontaneous efforts and were not rendered under any promise of compensation or reward.

"I am of course, grateful to all my friends in Georgia who participated in organizing clubs in my behalf. The action of Mr. Summers is, so far as I know, the only one in the United States to seek pecuniary gain or compensation."

This was replied to by a press statement by Mr. Summers:

May 25, 1932.

F. B. Summers, executive chairman of the Roosevelt Southern Clubs, who is expected to announce his candidacy for Governor of Georgia early next week, today criticized Governor Franklin D. Roosevelt for a statement the Governor gave out here today on his way from Warm Springs to New York. The statement referred to the suit of Summers to recover $6,540 that Summers alleges he and others advanced for the Roosevelt campaign in the South and Southwest. It was filed in the U. S. Court here last week. Mr. Summers said:

"In the last paragraph of his statement Governor Roosevelt said:

" 'I am of course grateful to my friends in Georgia who participated in organizing clubs in my behalf. The action of Mr. Summers is, as far as I know, the only one in the United States to seek pecuniary gain or compensation.'

"This is a bold attempt," declared Summers in this statement, "to confuse the public mind concerning this suit. We are not seeking any 'pecuniary gain or compensation' from Mr. Roosevelt. We are merely suing him to force him to refund the money we advanced on his authorization and that of his manager, James A. Farley, chairman of the New York Democratic Committee, for his campaign, managed by us, to secure Roosevelt delegates in 17 Southern and Southwestern States, which we vigorously carried on and very successfully, too, for more than fourteen months. We caused the organization of hundreds of Roosevelt-for-President Clubs in more than one-third of the United States, secured the support of leaders of the powerful Ku Klux Klan, and successfully organized this territory for his candidacy. We received his thanks for this work, profusely, in writing and per-

179

sonally at Warm Springs, but so far he and Farley have failed to pay the actual expenses of this campaign, guaranteed by them to us.

"We are not asking any 'pecuniary gain or compensation' from Mr. Roosevelt yet. And we haven't got around to Mr. Farley yet.

"The paragraph is in line with Governor Roosevelt's usual policy of sidestepping an issue and coincides with his custom of dodging any important questions. In this instance, however, he has attempted to deceive the public as to the real issue of the suit. That's the very reason why so many important democratic leaders are against him—he won't stay put, and he will throw down a friend without compunction.

"His race for delegates has been a 'beggar's campaign' for he has bamboozled credulous citizens into working for him and got them to also pay the expenses of this work. In Georgia some one paid his primary entrance fee of $1,000. We will let the U. S. Court decide whether he pays or also 'works us for suckers.'

"However, we cannot blame him very much, for the Dutch were ever a close-fisted race and ever anxious to get something for nothing."

The suit created quite a stir and because of the publicity was hurting Roosevelt's chances for the presidential nomination. In a short time Summers and others in the Clubs were induced to withdraw the suit on promise that the claim would be paid by either Roosevelt or Farley. The suit was withdrawn several months before the Chicago convention that nominated Roosevelt.

180

The money was never paid. Thus Roosevelt and Farley pulled a double "gyp" on Summers and his associates.

At the time of the suit Attorney J. Ira Harrelson was President of the Atlanta Board of Education, and a lawyer considered one of the leaders of the Atlanta bar.

Summers afterward ran for Governor of Georgia, but withdrew because of illness before the State primary, in favor of Eugene Talmadge, who was nominated and elected.

It was reported that because of the suit Roosevelt and Farley used their influence in Georgia against Summers, candidate for governor.

The Klan is now, however, opposed to many policies of the Roosevelt Administration. When the Roosevelt pre-nomination campaign started in 1931 in Atlanta the Klan was redhot for Roosevelt's nomination. This was shown, as described elsewhere, by the former general counsel of the Klan, Judge Paul S. Etheridge, acting as chairman of the Roosevelt-for-President Clubs, and the loan of the Klan furniture for the Roosevelt clubs headquarters in Atlanta.

At present it may be stated with authority that Klansmen everywhere are in a vast majority opposed to the Roosevelt Administration. This is caused by the fact that many, very many, of the Washington administrative offices, some of great importance are filled by Jews. There is a suspicion among Klansmen that among this aggregation many are tainted with Communism or Fascism, and this suspicion has since been confirmed by the report

181

of the Dies Committee. Charles Michelson, publicity director of the Democratic National Committee, is a Jew. He is the only Jew ever to be elected to membership in the famed Washington Gridiron Club, where Jews as members have always been barred. This membership shows how Jewry has invaded official Washington and even entered the sacred Gridiron Club. And in passing, it may be stated that negroes are barred from the Congressional Press Galleries. The Klansmen believe that Jews and Catholics, in official Washington positions, are out of all proportion to Protestants and Gentiles.

The appointment of Myron C. Taylor as President Roosevelt"s ambassador to the Vatican has, it is reported in Atlanta, further alienated every Klansman in the United States, who are alarmed at what they consider Roosevelt's first move to more firmly entrench the Catholic Church in the American government.

Democracy, weekly Georgia newspaper, in an editorial on January 11, 1940, with approval it is said of prominent Atlanta Klansmen, among whom are some of Georgia's leading citizens, had this to say about the Taylor ambassadorship:

"In naming Myron C. Taylor as his 'personal representative' to the Vatican, President Roosevelt has made another colossal blunder.

"Whether this be just another stupid innovation, suggested by the Communistic crowd of crackpots that advise Roosevelt, or whether it be the beginning of a subtle scheme by those hidden in the shadow of the White House to eventually have an accredited and Senate confirmed ambassador, remains to be seen.

"This appointment puts the United States through the back door into international religious politics, for none can deny that the Vatican is a political power. It is more meddling in European affairs, and brings us nearer to war with Russia and Germany. The President would not have dared to submit this nomination to the Senate for confirmation.

An ambassador is always a personal representative of a sovereign power. Taylor is such, with rank of ambassador and pay, except that he has not been confirmed by the Senate. Just another usurpation of Constitutional powers by Roosevelt. The United States in fact now has an ambassador to the Pope. The Senate has been ignored.

"There is absolutely no need for Roosevelt to collaborate with Pius Twelfth in this European conflict. The Pope, a splendid old statesman, is doing all he can to bring peace, and so is Roosevelt, vocally and apparently. What strength is a partnership between Roosevelt and the Vatican for peace? None.

"The United States is a temporal power. The Vatican is supposed to be a spiritual power. In our country, Church and State are separated. The Taylor appointment tends to destroy this.

"We wonder if the hand of Jim Farley is not back of this matter, of the attempt to involve the United States in the meshes of the Catholic Church in European affairs, and eventually in the United States. A year or so ago

Farley had a long interview with Pius Twelfth, kissed the Pope's toe in fealty, and received medals from His Holiness for himself and members of his family.

"All good citizens abhor bringing a religious or an intolerance issue into political affairs, or of government, but when a President of the United States begins a scheme to change, ever so slightly, our traditional policy of church and state it is time for all real Americans to protest. There are plenty of good Catholics and loyal Americans who will deplore this White House blunder.

"The Roosevelt letters announcing the appointment slop over with unctious sentiments and manifestly are a bid for support from not only Catholics and Jews but Protestants. Some Protestant leaders and ministers have publicly objected to the appointment.

"It is the most dangerous thing that Roosevelt has done to destroy the Democratic Party, which he has already set well on the road to national socialism.

The country is afflicted with too much Roosevelt.

"No Pope or crown

Shall rule this town."

CHAPTER XXII

THE KLAN TAKES OFF THE MASK

In March and April, 1940, a number of night-whippings by alleged Klansmen occurred in East Point, a suburb of Atlanta, becoming public by the discovery of the body of Ike Gaston, a barber, who had been flogged to death, or who had died as a result of a beating received the same night. Finding of the body caused an immediate investigation by legal authorities of Fulton County, and by officials of the headquarters of the Klan in Atlanta, headed by Imperial Wizard Colescott.

A grand jury investigation developed the fact that about fifty such meetings, by alleged Klansmen or other lawless men not Klansmen, had taken place in Fulton county for some years past, the victims failing to report the assaults, for fear of reprisals. These victims and several hundred witnesses were examined by the Grand Jury, a large number of indictments returned, and a number of persons arrested and tried. It developed that deputy sheriffs were alleged participants in some of the outrages, and these were suspended from office, pending their trials.

Imperial Wizard Colescott announced that any Klansmen guilty of such crimes would be expelled from the Order. He appeared before the Grand Jury several times and cooperated in every possible way with the investigation.

The second Congressional investigation of the Klan, in Simmons' time, was precipitated by a similar occurrence in 1920, in Louisiana, where it was alleged Klansmen, or scoundrels posing as Klansmen, had beaten scores of persons at night, and in one instance murdered several victims by running heavy road building machinery over them. This was never proved, however, but was one of the principal causes of the Congressional investigation.

While the trials of the persons indicted for the alleged night-ridings and floggings in Fulton County were going on a movement started in Atlanta, by persons opposed to the Klan, to cause another Congressional investigation. At the time this book was written, however, nothing definite had developed toward a new Congressional investigation.

During Reconstruction times some of the Southern States passed strong legislation forbidding the Klan or similar organizations to exist.

In 1927 New York State passed an anti-Klan law. This was six years after the second Congressional investigation. On November 19, 1928, the United States Supreme Court declared the Klan to be an undesirable organization. The decision was handed down by Associate Justice Van Devanter, all the justices concurring except Justice McReynolds. The decision upheld the New York anti-Klan law. Justice McReynold's dissenting opinion held that the U. S. Supreme Court had no jurisdiction over the case.

A number of other attempts were made at that time

or afterwards by various States to forbid the Klan operating in these states, without result, however.

The principal objection to the Ku Klux Klan has always been that its membership appeared in public masked, and so disguised that the public could not know who the members were.

The use of masks had also been used in night-riding, floggings, and other outrages.

The necessity of doing away with masks was considered even in the Simmons administration, but the masks were retained.

In 1928, during the Evans regime, caused largely by the U. S. Supreme Court decision, an attempt was made by high Klan officers to have the membership unmask. At this time the second degree of the Order, the "Knights of the Great Forest" was established. All who took this degree were ordered to discard the masks. However, a great number of members did not take the degree, and these retained their masks.

The disclosures and the publicity concerning the Fulton County outrages and the Gaston death, coupled with the policy of the new Imperial Wizard, Colescott, to abolish as much secrecy from the Order as possible, led to a meeting in Atlanta the week of April 14, 1940, of the national Kloncilium of the Klan, that is the state heads or national governing body of the Klan, from all States. The Kloncilium, under the leadership of Imperial Wizard Colescott, ordered that the mask of every member of the Klan be immitaely removed, never to be used again.

It also restricted use of the Fiery Cross, and put a strict curb on future Klan parades and demonstrations of every kind. Immediately after this meeting of the Kloncilium adjourned Imperial Wizard Colescott issued two edicts, the first restricting burning of fiery crosses, and the other restricting Klan parades, and abolishing the mask.

Colescott announced that many Klans, in the East and Mid West, had never used the mask, and that some Klans before the meeting had voluntarily discontinued use of the mask. Colescott stated that he had been considering banishing the mask ever since he had been elected Imperial Wizard, in June, 1939.

In issuing the edicts, Colescott sent imperative orders to all Klans through the United States, to collect and destroy any Klan helmets which have masks.

Heretofore, masked parades and burning of fiery crosses have sometimes preceded alleged Klan whippings and night-ridings.

The edicts made public on April 17, are as follows:

"The imperial Kloncilium, the national board of directors of the Knights of the Ku Klux Klan, convened in annual session at the imperial headquarters here Saturday, April 14, and continued in session until early Wednesday, discussing matters governing the policy and the general operation of our organization.

"Among the many matters which were considered there were two which appeared to be of interest to the general public. I, therefore, am releasing to the press copies of two official edicts which are being promulgated immediately.

188

" 'Since I became imperial wizard, in June of last year, I have traveled throughout at least a third of the states of the nation, conferring with Klan leaders and visiting local Klans in order that I might acquaint myself with the various conditions existing in every section of the country, so as to be of greater service to my organization.

"In reporting to the Kloncilium my findings, I recommended, among other things, that the position of the Klan regarding public appearances, the use of the robe, the helmet and the fiery cross be definitely stated. In order to accomplish this, I prepared two edicts and presented them to the kloncilium, which, after thorough discussion, unanimously approved them and recommended that they be made public.

"The first edict refers to the fiery cross.

"The fiery cross, the official emblem of the Knights of the Ku Klux Klan, is a sacred symbol, emblematic of the cross upon which Christ, the Klansman's criterion of character, was crucified. Under the fiery cross every Klansman assumes his most solemn obligation and consecrates himself to a life of service and sacrifice for the right. For this reason the fiery cross may be used only as I have outlined in this edict.

"The robe or official costume of the Klan is distinctive and contains deep significance for a Klansman. Therefore, in the second edict, I have defined the only conditions under which the official costume of the Klan may be used in public.

"With reference to the helmet, I have prescribed the only type of helmet permissible for use with the official costume of the Klan, from which the mask or visor has been eliminated.

"In addition to this edict, I am immediately notifying every Klan leader in the nation to collect and destroy any helmet, either in the Klavern or in the possession of any Klansman, which may bear a mask or visor, in order that there shall be no possibility of any Klansman appearing in public or private with his face hidden by a mask."

Unmasking of the Klan met the general approbation of rightminded citizens and generally of the Georgia press. The Atlanta Journal, one of the South's leading newspapers, said editorially, following announcement of the Imperial edicts:

"The unmasking of the Ku Klux Klan, announced Wednesday by its national officials, comes as welcome news to every friend of law and order. Henceforth, according to edicts issued by James A. Colescott, imperial wizard, members of the Klan are forbidden, under penalty of expulsion, to wear the hooded visor either in public or in private. Nor shall Klansmen in the altered costume participate in any parade or other demonstration without permission from the higher officials of their order and from the public authorities as well. The burning of the 'fiery cross' is likewise prohibited except under the sanction of the higher officials and with the consent of the owner of the property where such a spectacle is to be staged.

"These long-needed reforms follow fast upon a grand jury probe which has implicated suburban units of the Ku Klux Klan in Fulton County in a series of brutal floggings. There are more than 50 known victims of this night-riding terrorism, one of whom, died from the lash of his persecutors. In justice to their organization as a whole the national leaders of the Ku Klux Klan were bound to take cognizance of such disclosures. They condemned the crimes and promised that any of their members convicted thereof should be banished from the 'empire.'

"That this view now is indorsed by the chief rulers of the Ku Klux Klan itself is more than gratifying. It is a token of good faith and honest purpose, a victory for aroused conscience and aroused intelligence, a substitution of light for darkness and of open dealing for dangerous concealment. 'Imperial Wizard Colescott announces that orders have gone forth to insure that there shall be no possibility of any Klansman appearing in public or private with his face hidden by a mask. It is fair to assume that every Klansman who is mindful of the good repute of his organization and the interests of the public will welcome this revolutionary order. If there be those who think otherwise, the question well may be asked: What lies in their hearts that they should wish their faces hidden?"

Most of the Fulton County outrages had been traced to alleged members of the East Point Klan No. 61, Realm of Georgia. On April 19 Imperial Wizard Colescott went to the hall of this Klan, took the charter off the wall,

191

gathered up all the records and regalia, including the robes and masks, and announced that this Klan was suspended pending the result of the criminal trials of those indicted, then proceeding in the Fulton County Superior Court. This Klan was one of the oldest in the organization and was reputed to have more than 500 members. It had been chartered November 12, 1920, during the administration of Imperial Wizard Simmons.

In suspending this Klan Colescott announced that some of the members were planning to intimidate witnesses against the defendants under indictment or trial. He issued the following statement, after seizing the material of this Klan, which he deposited in the Imperial Palace headquarters at Buckhead:

"Obviously this Klan, or at any rate some of its members, have failed to respect the usuages of the order. The Ku Klux Klan does not stand for outlawry.

"This Klan has a membership of about 500, and I am certain that the vast majority are decent, honorable members.

"The few trouble-makers are like a handful of rotten apples in a barrel of sound fruit. When this whipping business is settled, and the rotten element has been kicked out and punished, I hope to reorganize East Point into a model Klan."

With the Klan unmasked, and it's parades and "fiery cross" demonstrations curbed, there is no reason now why it should not become, as it was twice, a great national organization of patriotic Americans, devoted to Americanism, and openly a vigorous foe of all the "isms" that now plague this country—a great patriotic society that is determined to stand for "America First," and for the things that make the United States with free speech, free press, free worship, free assembly, and the Bill of Rights, the greatest country in the whole wide world.

That Atlanta and Fulton County officials do not blame the Klan as an organization for the recent night-riding outrages is shown by the following letter from the Fulton County Grand Jury that indicted 17 of the perpetrators of these crimes, sent to Imperial Wizard Colescott.

FULTON COUNTY GRAND JURY

March-April Term, 1940

Mr. J. A. Colescott, Imperial Wizard
Knights of the Ku Klux Klan,
3155 Roswell Road, N.E.
Atlanta, Ga.
Dear Sir:

Traditionally, dating back to the days of the Magna Charta, the Grand Jury has been described as "the people acting on their own." In that sense and for that reason we are naturally appreciative when any citizen acts to cooperate with our body for the good of the community.

This Grand Jury has been greatly impressed by your evident sincerity and your willing cooperation in matters involving acts of individuals and groups of individuals in the East Point sector of Fulton County—acts seemingly emanating from organization made possible by membership association in a unit of your fraternal body.

We recognize fully the difficulties attendant to control of any national organization with hundreds of units scat-

193

tered over the separate states. We appreciate that a given group in one such unit may engage in some illegal or unlawful action which would not be approved or condoned by the national governing body. In no sense would we take the action of such a group as an indictment against the order as a whole.

We can and do expect that when such a condition is made evident to the governing authorities that they will take such action as lies within their power in the matter of disciplining those who appear to be involved.

All this and more you have done willingly and on your own volition. You have appeared at sacrifice to your own interest to furnish and explain records desired by this body.

You have voluntarily removed the Charter and suspended the East Point unit, pending the final outcome of investigations and prosecutions now being or to be carried forward.

While not exactly part of the incidents pertinent to this Grand Jury, we believe you have taken an action for your own organization and meeting with the approval of all thinking citizens that you have ordered the removal of the visor from all Klan regalia.

Being even quicker to commend than we are to condemn, we desire to express on behalf of the people we represent, our deep appreciation of your splendid attitude and your fine cooperation in all matters affecting this Grand Jury and its relation to your organization.

Sincerely yours,

KENDALL WEISIGER,
Foreman

A Klansman's Song

E. N. S.   E. N. Sanctuary

1. We gath - er here as Klans-men true, No sel - fish plan have we,
2. To - day we hear our coun-try's call, It is an ur - gent cry,
3. A - rouse ye sons of wor-thy sires, Ne'er stop to count the cost,

When lib - er - ty shall call to us, We'll heed her faint-est plea;
In ev - 'ry hour, in ev - 'ry need, She'll al - ways find us nigh;
The rights our Con - sti - tu - tion gave, To - mor - row may be lost;

For home and God and coun-try dear, We'll close the Klansman's ranks,
For we have sworn, our oath did take, Our fier - y cross did burn,
No sac - ri - fice is made in vain, When we our laws de - fend,

For bless-ings here so rich - ly found, We give to God our thanks.
All a - lien ways we would op - pose, False lead - er-ship would spurn.
Our form - er rights we wish re-stored, God's light on us de - scend.

APPENDIX A.

Conditions under Reconstruction.

With the negroes newly enfranchised and the Southern State governments in the hands of corrupt carpetbaggers from the North and native scalawags, with insolent and ignorant negro militia swarming in nearly every county, and with bad economic conditions in the prostrate South, coupled with the disorder that always occur in every country after a devastating war, the native population of the South had much to complain of.

Corrupt government in each Southern State, oppression of the people by the agents of the Freedman's Bureau, thousands of criminal negroes armed and newly released from slavery, roaming around and committing murders, arsons and rapes, had got the Southern people down. But they did not stay down long.

A spark was lighted at Pulaski, Tennessee, when the first Klan organized, and soon the Klan rose like a flame in every section of the South, put down crime, punished criminals, ran the carpetbaggers away, and in a few years recaptured white political supremacy, established law and order, and made the beginning of a New South. The negro militia was disarmed and abolished. Carpetbag governors were either defeated or forced to flee their states, as in the case of Governor Bullock, of Georgia.

196

On December 5, 1870, President Grant sent a special message to Congress, in which he declared that the "free exercise of franchise has by violence and intimidation been denied to citizens in several of the States lately in rebellion." Senator Morton in a Senate resolution called on the President for definite information of the disorders in the South, and on January 13 the President submitted to the Senate a list of about 5,000 cases of alleged disorders, outrages and homicides in the Southern States. All of these alleged cases were of course supplied the President by carpetbag governors, agents of the Freedman's Bureau and U. S. military officers in command of the Southern districts.

Following this information a select Senate committee was appointed and sent a sub-committee to North Carolina to investigate the reports of disorders in that State. This commiteee made its report to the Senate on March 10. The majority report declared that the Klan did exist and was indulging in intimidation and even murders, but the minority report declared that the reports of such disorders had been "grossly and wilfully exaggerated."

Following this report President Grant sent a message calling on Congress to take some action.

Congress then enacted the law entitled: "An Act to enforce the provision of the Fourteenth Amendment to the Constitution of the United States, and for other purposes." On April 7 Congress passed a resolution "to inquire into the condition of the late insurrectionary States." A resolution was adopted for appointment of a select

197

committee to make the investigation, and this committee was soon appointed. It included seven senators and fourteen representatives.

The senators were: John Scott, chairman, R., Pa.; Zachariah Chandler, R., Mich.; Benjamin F. Rice, R., Ark.; T. F. Bayard, D., Del.; Frank P. Blair, D., Mo.; John Pool, R., N. C.; and Daniel D. Pratt, R., Ind.

The Representatives included: Luke P. Poland, chairman, R., Vt.; Horace Maynard, R., Tenn.; Glenni W. Schofield, R., Pa.; Burton C. Cook, R., Ill.; John Coburn, R., Ind.; Job E. Stevenson, R., Ohio; Charles W. Buckley, D., Ala.; William E. Lansing, R., N. Y.; Samuel S. Cox, D., Ohio; James B. Beck, D., Ky.; Daniel W. Voorhees, D., Ind.; Philadelphia, D., Ill.

During the hearings Buckley, Cook, and Voorhees retired from the committee and were succeeded by John F. Farnsworth, R., Ill.; Benjamin F. Butler, R., Mass.; and James M. Hanks, D., Ark.

Thirteen of the committee were Republicans and eight were Democrats.

This committee held numerous hearings in Washington and sub-committees made investigations in the Southern States. Many hundreds of witnesses were examined.

This committee published thirteen volumes of the hearings.

General Forrest was one of the witnesses before the committee but his testimony was vague and his answers to questions concerning the Klan were considered of no value to the committee. Other very prominent Southern men were examined, many former officers in the Confederate Army, and hundreds of ignorant negroes were on the witness stand.

When the sub-committee investigating North Carolina conditions completed its work the majority report said "The Ku Klux does exist and it had political purposes which it sought to carry out by murders, whippings, intimidation and violence."

The minority report said that the alleged outrages had been "grossly and wilfully exaggerated and that no act of violence had been proven except in six, perhaps eight, of the eighty-seven North Carolina counties."

Both reports were undoubtedly colored by politics.

A sub-committee investigating conditions in South Carolina reported that revolutionary conditions existed in that State, and Chairman Scott wrote to President Grant urging the President to take some action.

Mr. Van Trump, however, in a minority report, declared that the disorders in South Carolina were "the natural offspring of as corrupt and oppressive a system of local State government as ever disgraced humanity, and utterly unparalled in the history of civilization."

The reports of investigations in all the other states by the Congressional sub-committees were largely similar, a majority report condemning the disorders, and a minority report denouncing the conditions of State and local governments which were the primary cause of the disorderly conditions and violence.

The hearings brought out the fact that the genuine Ku Klux organizations in every Southern State, practically without exception, were simply acting as citizens' law and order committees to put down disorder and lawlessness, and it was known that the best class of Southern citizens were members. These klans undoubtedly whipped bad negroes or white men, warned others out of neighborhood, ran obnoxious carpetbagger and scalawags away, and in some cases executed criminals that were guilty of murder, arson, rape, and all kinds of crime.

In several States the genuine Klans actually fought pitched battles with negro militia companies, and organizations of negroes or carpetbaggers and nearly always came off victorious.

In the disordered conditions in the South many vicious and criminal characters took advantage of the Klan's disguises and using similar regalia committees outrages which were laid to the door of the Klan. In many instances the genuine Klansmen, when they could get the evidence, caught and ran out of the country the spurious Klansmen masquerading as genuine Klansmen, and in other cases simply executed the scoundrels after fair trials. Many a criminal negro, carpetbagger or scalawag, simply disappeared from his haunts, and was seen no more. There were dozens of these cases, but the times were desperate and required desperate remedies.

As a matter of fact, to an impartial investigator, the old Ku Klux Klan saved white civilization in the South, achieved the social and political ascendancy of the white race, and reestablished a reign of law, which has endured to this day in the South.

APPENDIX B.

Attorney General Gregory's Statement.

In an address before the Bar Association of Texas in 1906, Hon. Thomas W. Gregory, later Attorney-General of the United States, gave a history of the old Klan, and in speaking of its work said:

"It is safe to say that ninety per cent of the work of the Klan involved no act of personal violence. In most instances mere knowledge of the fact that the Ku Klux were organized in the community and patrolled it by night accomplished most that was desired. In the case of nocturnal meetings of the negroes, organized by scalawags and carpetbaggers, which proved disorderly and offensive, sheeted horsemen would be found drawn up across every road leading from the meeting place; and although not a word was spoken and no violence whatever offered, that meeting was usually adjourned sine die. . . . But masked riders and mystery were not the only Ku Klux devices. Carpetbaggers and scalawags and their families were ostracized in all walks of life—in the church, in the school, in business, wherever men and women or even children gathered together, no matter what the purpose or the place, the alien and the renegade, and all that belonged or pertained to them were refused recognition and consigned to outer darkness and the companionship of negroes.

"In addition to these methods, there were some of a much more drastic nature. The sheeted horseman did not merely warn and intimidate, especially when the warnings were not heeded. In many instances negroes and carpet-baggers were whipped and in rare instances shot or hanged. Notice to leave the country was frequently extended and rarely declined, and if declined the results were likely to be serious. Hanging was promptly administered to the house burner and sometimes to the murderer; the defamer of women of good character was usually whipped and sometimes executed if the offense was repeated; threats of violence and oppression of the weak and defenseless if persisted in after due warning met with drastic and sometimes cruel remedies; mere corruption in public office was too universal for punishment or even comment, but he who prostituted official power to oppress the individual, a crime prevalent from one end of the country to the other, especially in cases where it affected the widow and orphan, was likely to be dealt with in no gentle way, in case a warning was not promptly observed; those who advocated and practiced social equality of the races and incited hostility of the blacks against the whites were given a single notice to depart in haste, and they rarely took time to reply."

In September, 1868, Governor Brownlow of Tennessee called the legislature into session, and caused a drastic act to be passed comparable only to the Reconstruction Acts of Congress. Under its terms association or connection with the Ku Klux Klan was punishable by a fine of $500 and imprisonment in the penitentiary for not less than five years. Any inhabitant of the State was constituted an officer possessing power to arrest without process any one known to be, or suspected of being, a member of the organization; and to feed, lodge or conceal a member was made a criminal offense punishable by fine and imprisonment, and informers were allowed one-half the fine. In spite of this drastic law, the Klan continued to actively operate in Tennessee for over six months.

Partly because of this law, and partly because of the fact that in many cases some of the "Dens" had gone beyond their instructions in coping with the situation, and were showing a tendency to get beyond the control of the men who were trying to conduct the movement honestly, but principally because the purpose of its regulation work had been accomplished and there remained no reason for its existence, General Forrest, in the latter part of February, 1869, issued a proclamation as Grand Wizard declaring the Ku Klux Klan dissolved and disbanded.

The substance of his order is included in his summary which reads:

"The Invisible Empire has accomplished the purpose for which it was organized. Civil law now affords ample protection to life, liberty and property; robbery and lawlessness are no longer unrebuked; the better elements of society are no longer in dread for the safety of their property, their persons, and their families. The Grand Wizard, being invested with power to determine questions of paramount importance, in the exercise of the power so conferred, now declares the Invisible Empire and all the subdivisions thereof dissolved and disbanded forever."

APPENDIX C.

Lieut. Gen. Nathan Bedford Forrest, Founder and First Head of the Ku Klux Klan.

Nathan Bedford Forrest, lieutenant general in the Armies of the Confederate States, and founder and first head of the Ku Klux Klan during Reconstruction days after the war between the States, was born near Chapel Hill, Tennessee, July 13, 1821. He received no formal education, but educated himself by reading and study and was noted as a mathematician. General Forrest became an educated man by his own reading and study, as a letter written by him proves in this chapter. For many years there has been a saying attributed to Forrest, regarding his military campaigns: "Git there fustest with the mostest men." It is not known who started this saying but it was a base canard. General Forrest by his own efforts rose from a poor, ignorant boy to be a great military commander, a polished gentleman and man of the world, at home in any company.

He was first a cattle and horse dealer in Mississippi, and then a slave and cattle dealer in Memphis, Tennessee. In 1849 he became a cotton planter in Mississippi and accumulated a large fortune.

In 1861 he volunteered in the Confederate Army as a private, soon raised a cavalry command, and was commissioned lieutenant colonel. In February, 1861, Fort Donelson was captured by General Grant. Generals Floyd and Pillow, in command of this fort, surrendered, but not Forrest. He forded the Mississippi river at night and escaped with his whole command. Next he participated in the Battle of Shiloh, was appointed a brigadier general of the Confederacy July, 1862, and put in command of a Confederate cavalry brigade, which made a great record as hard riders and fighters.

While serving under General Bragg, Forrest surrounded and forced the surrender of an entire brigade of Federal Cavalry commanded by Col. A. D. Streight, U.S. Army. This was in April, 1863. Forrest and his troopers participated in the bloody battle of Chicamauga, September, 1863, and he was commissioned a major general December, 1863. April 12, 1864, he stormed and captured Fort Pillow, on the Mississippi river, in Tennessee. This was largely garrisoned by Federal negro troops and a great many of them were killed in the assault. It was claimed in the North that these negro troops were massacred after some of them surrendered, but Forrest always asserted that this was not true; that all troops who threw down their arms as the Confederates stormed the fort were protected and treated according to the rules of civilized warfare. On June 10, 1864, he defeated a large Federal force at Brice's Cross Roads, in Mississippi, and then raided thru Mississippi, Tennessee, and Alabama, harassing Federal commands and capturing supply trains. February, 1865, he was commissioned lieutenant general. May 9, 1865, he surrendered with his command to General James H. Wilson, U.S. Army, at Selma, Alabama, the war between the States being practically over and the Confederacy defeated.

After the war General Forrest made his home in Memphis, Tennessee, and became president of the Selma, Marion & Memphis Railroad. He died in Memphis, October 29, 1877, aged 56 years.

Capt. John Morton, of Nashville, Tenn., was chief of artillery for Forrest during practically the entire war between the States. The author in 1900 was connected with a Nashville daily newspaper and Captain Morton, then Secretary of State of Tennessee, was his good friend. Captain Morton often recounted to the author his stirring days with Forrest and repeatedly asserted that Forrest was the organizer and originator of the Ku Klux Klan. Captain Morton should have known as he was an intimate friend of Forrest and himself head of the Nashville Klan during Reconstruction days.

Forrest was described by Captain Morton as a large, handsome man of very imposing appearance and bearing, of great intelligence, and fine education.

Morton said that Forrest, in every battle, personally, sabre in hand, led every charge and every attack, that he personally engaged in sabre duels with the enemy whenever possible and was a man absolutely without fear. Stories that Forrest was an illiterate were denounced by Captain Morton as "infernal lies" and if anybody wanted to arouse this old veteran's fighting ire he had only to say something derogatory about Forrest.

Forrest spent the last years of his life in working his plantation. He met with such success that he not only made a good living but was able to help many needy Confederate soldiers and families of soldiers. He shared his income with them, and after his death his wife kept up the good work with great generosity, spending most of the fortune Forrest left her.

Forrest was a devoted father as well as husband. In April, 1865, when full of anxiety about the future, he wrote his son the following letter:

Gainesville, Ala.,
April 15, 1865.

Lieut. Wm. M. Forrest:
My dear Son:

Loving you with all the affection which a fond father can bestow upon a dutiful son, I deem it my duty to give you a few words of advice. Life, as you know, is uncertain at best, and occupying the position I do it is exceedingly hazardous. I may fall at any time, or I may, at no distant day, be an exile in a foreign land, and I desire to address you a few words, which I trust you will remember through life.

You have heretofore been an obedient, dutiful son. You have given your parents but little pain or trouble, and I hope you will strive to profit by any suggestions I may make. I have had a full understanding with your mother as to our future operations in the event the enemy overruns the country. She will acquaint you with our plans and will look to you in the hour of trouble. Be to her a prop and support; she is worthy of all the love you bestow upon her. I know how devoted you are to her, but study her happiness and above and beyond all things, give her no cause for unhappiness. Try to emulate her noble virtues and practice her blameless life. If I have been wicked and sinful myself, it would rejoice my heart to see you leading the Christian life which has adorned your mother.

What I most desire of you, my son, is never to gamble or swear. These are baneful vices, and I trust you will never practice either. As I grow older I see the folly of these two vices, and beg that you will never engage in them. Your life heretofore has been elevated and characterized by a high-toned morality, and I trust your name will never be stained by the practice of those vices which have blighted the prospects of some of the most prominent youth of our country.

Be honest, be truthful, in all your dealings with the world. Be cautious in the selection of your friends. Shun the society of the low and vulgar. Strive to elevate your character and to take a high and honorable position in society. You are my only child, the pride and hope of my life. You have fine intellect, talent of the highest order. I have watched your entrance upon the threshold of manhood and life with all the admiration of a proud father, and I trust your future career will be an honor to yourself and a solace to my declining years. If we meet no more on earth, I hope you will keep this letter prominently before you and remember it as coming from
Your affectionate father,
N. B. Forrest.

Ten years after the war the general's health gave way. The four hard years of struggle had undermined his iron strength. He had marched and fought and worked for days and nights at a time, giving himself wholly to the cause he served. He now had to pay the price of overwork.

As his health failed, Forrest changed greatly. Hot-tempered, wilful, strong in body and mind as he had always been, he was, nevertheless, a very tender man. This tenderness came out in him with the approach of death. General Wheeler said of him about this time: "Every suggestion of harshness had gone from his face, and he seemed to have in these last days the gentleness of expression, the voice and manner of a woman."

He joined the church not long before the end. He said to General John T. Morgan: "General, I am broken in health and in spirit, and have not long to live. My life has been a battle from the start. It was a fight to make a livelihood for those dependent on me in my younger days, and an independence for myself when I grew up to manhood, as well as in the terrible struggle of the Civil War. I have seen too much of violence, and I want to close my days at peace with all the world, as I am now at peace with my Maker."

Forrest's last appearance in public was at a reunion of the Seventh Tennessee cavalry, on September 21, 1877. He was called on for a speech as he sat his horse, and, without dismounting, he made a talk to his men:

"Soldiers of the Seventh Tennessee cavalry, ladies, and gentlemen: I name the soldiers first because I love them best. I am very much pleased to meet them here to-day. I love the gallant men with whom I served in the war. You can hardly realize what must pass through a commander's mind when called upon to meet in reunion the brave spirits, who, through four years of war and bloodshed, fought fearlessly for a cause that they thought right, and who, even when they foresaw, as we did, that the war must close in disaster, yet did not quail but fought as boldly and stubbornly in their last battles as in their first.

"Nor do I forget those gallant spirits who sleep coldly in death upon the many bloody battlefields of the war. I love them, too, and honor their memory. I have often been called to the side of those who had been struck down in the battle, and they would put their arms around my neck, draw me down to them and say, 'General, I have fought my last battle and will soon be gone. I want you to remember my wife and children and take care of them.' Comrades, I have remembered their wives and little ones and have taken care of them, and I want every one of you to remember them also and join with me in the labor of love.

"Comrades, through the years of bloodshed and weary marches, you were tried and true soldiers. So through the years of peace you have been good citizens; and now that we are again united under the old flag, I love it as I did in the days of my youth, and I feel sure that you also love it. Yes, I love and honor the old flag as much as those who followed it on the other side; and I am sure that I but express your feelings when I say that should our country demand our services, you would follow me to battle as eagerly under that banner as ever you followed me in our late war."

"Forrest was not the man to grieve or repine because he had fought on the losing side in a great war. He had done his best for the South — no one had done better — but the South had failed to gain a place among the nations. Since this was so, Forrest was willing to become a loyal citizen of the United States and give his best efforts to build up the wasted land."

Professor H. J. Eckenrode in his "Life of Nathan B. Forrest" relates how General Forrest, when constructing a railroad from Selma, Alabama, to the Mississippi River, quarreled with a contractor which resulted in a challenge to fight a duel. General Forrest told a friend he was sure he could kill the man and if he did he would never forgive himself. "General Forrest," said the friend, "your courage has never been questioned. If I were you I would feel it my duty to apologize." "You are right," said Forrest, "I will do it." He sought the man he was about to fight, told him he was in the wrong, and shook hands with him. There was no duel. Forrest never did a braver thing than this, for it takes a great courage to admit being in the wrong.

Forrest's death caused great grief throughout the South and especially in the States he had defended in so many battles and marches. Ex-President Davis and other noted Confederates came to his funeral and followed his body to its resting place in beautiful Elmwood Cemetery. As they drove along in the funeral procession, Governor

Porter, of Tennessee, said to Mr. Davis: "History has given to General Forrest the first place as a cavalry leader in the War between the States and has named him as one of the half dozen great soldiers of the country."

"I agree," replied Mr. Davis, "the truth was that the generals commanding in the southwest never saw what was in Forrest until too late. Their judgment was that he was a bold raider and rider. I was misled by them and I never knew how to measure him until I read the reports of his movements across the Tennessee River in 1864."

General Sherman said of him: "After all, I think Forrest was the most remarkable man the Civil War produced on either side. In the first place, he was uneducated while Jackson and Sherman and other leaders were soldiers by calling. He never read a military book in his life, but he had a genius for war. There was no way by which I could tell what Forrest was up to. He seemed to know what I intended to do, while I am free to confess I could never tell what he was trying to do."

Lord Wolsley, the English general, said: "Forrest fought like a knight-errant for the cause he believed to be that of justice and right. No man who drew the sword for his country in that struggle deserves better of her; and as long as the deeds of her sons find poets to describe them and fair women to sing about them, the name of this gallant general will be remembered with love and admiration."

APPENDIX C.-C.

An Interview with General Forrest.

On August 28, 1868, there was printed in the Cincinnati Commercial an interview by a traveling correspondent with the celebrated Confederate Lieut. Gen. N. B. Forrest, then generally recognized as Grand Wizard of the Ku Klux Klan. This interview said, in part:

"Today I have enjoyed 'big talks' enough to have gratified any of the famous Indian chiefs who have been treating with General Sherman for the past two years. First I met General N. B. Forrest, then General Gideon A. Pillow, and Governor Isham G. Harris. My first visit was to General Forrest, whom I found at his office, at 8 o'clock this morning. Now that the southern people have elevated him to the position of their great leader and oracle, it may not be amiss to preface my conversation with him with a brief sketch of the gentleman.

"I cannot better personally describe him than by borrowing the language of one of his biographers. 'In person he is six feet one inch and a half in height, with broad shoulders, a full chest, and symmetrical, muscular limbs; erect in carriage, and weighs one hundred and eighty-five pounds; dark-gray eyes, dark hair, mustache and beard worn upon the chin; a set of regular white teeth, and clearly cut features'; which, altogether make him rather a handsome man for one forty-seven years of age.

Previous to the war—in 1852—he left the business of planter, and came to this city and engaged in the business of 'negro trader,' in which traffic he seems to have been quite successful, for, by 1861, he had become the owner of two plantations a few miles below here, in Mississippi, on which he produced about a thousand bales of cotton each year, in the meantime carrying on the negro-trading. In June, 1861, he was authorized by Governor Harris, of Tennessee, to recruit a regiment of cavlary for the war, which he did, and which was the nucleus around which he gathered the army which he commanded as lieutenant general at the end of the war.

After being seated in his office, I said:

'General Forrest, I came especially to learn your views in regard to the condition of your civil and political affairs in the State of Tennessee, and the South generally. I desire them for publication in the Cincinnati Commercial. I do not wish to misinterpret you in the slightest degree, and therefore only ask for such views as you are willing I should publish.'

'I have not now,' he replied, 'and never have had, any opinion on any public or political subject which I would object to having published. I mean what I say, honestly and earnestly, and only object to being misrepresented. I dislike to be placed before the country in a false position, especially as I have not sought the reputation I have gained.'

I replied: 'Sir, I will publish only what you say, and then you can not possibly be misrepresented. Our people desire to know your feelings toward the General Government, the State government of Tennessee, the radical party, both in and out of the State, and upon the question of negro suffrage.'

'Well, sir,' said he, 'when I surrendered my seven thousand men in 1865, I accepted a parole honestly, and I have observed it faithfully up to today. I have counseled peace in all the speeches I have made. I have advised my people to submit to the laws of the State, oppressive as they are, and unconstitutional as I believe them to be. I was paroled and not pardoned until the issuance of the last proclamation of general amnesty; and, therefore, did not think it prudent for me to take any active part until the oppression of my people became so great that they could not endure it, and then I would be with them.

'Then, I suppose, general, that you think the oppression has become so great that your people should no longer bear it.'

'No,' he answered, 'It is growing worse hourly, yet I have said to the people, 'Stand fast, let us try to right the wrong by legislation.' A few weeks ago I was called to Nashville to counsel with other gentlemen who had been prominently identified with the cause of the confederacy, and we then offered pledges which we thought would be satisfactory to Mr. Brownlow and his legislature, and we told them that, if they would not call out the militia, we would agree to preserve order and see that

215

the laws were enforced. The legislative committee certainly led me to believe that our proposition would be accepted and no militia organized. Believing this, I came home, and advised all of my people to remain peaceful, and to offer no resistance to any reasonable law. It is true that I never have recognized the present government in Tennessee as having any legal existence, yet I was willing to submit to it for a time, with the hope that the wrongs might be righted peaceably.'

'What are your feelings towards the Federal Government, general?'

'I loved the old Government in 1861; I love the Constitution yet. I think it is the best government in the world if administered as it was before the war. I do not hate it; I am opposing now only the radical revolutionists who are trying to destroy it. I believe that party to be composed, as I know it is in Tennessee, of the worst men on God's earth—men who would hesitate at no crime, and who have only one object in view, to enrich themselves.'

'In the event of Governor Brownlow's calling out the militia, do you think there will be any resistance offered to their acts?' I asked.

'That will depend upon circumstances. If the militia are simply called out, and do not interfere with or molest any one, I do not think there will be any fight. If, on the contrary, they do what I believe they will do, commit outrages, or even one outrage, upon the people, they and Mr. Brownlow's government will be swept out of existence; not a radical will be left alive. If the militia are called out, we can not but look upon it as a declaration of war, because Mr. Brownlow has already issued his proclamation directing them to shoot down the Ku Klux wherever they find them; and he calls all southern men Ku Klux.'

'Why, general, we people up north have regarded the Ku Klux as an organization which existed only in the frightened imaginations of a few politicians.'

'Well, sir, there is such an organization, not only in Tennessee but all over the South, and its numbers have not been exaggerated.'

'What are its numbers, general?'

'In Tennessee there are over forty thousand; in all the Southern States about five hundred and fifty thousand men.'

'What is the character of the organization, may I inquire?'

'Yes, sir. It is a protective, political, military organization. I am willing to show any man the constitution of the society. The members are sworn to recognize the Government of the United States. It does not say anything at all about the government of the State of Tennessee. Its objects originally were protection against Loyal Leagues and the Grand Army of the Republic; but after it became general it was found that political matters and interests could best be promoted within it, and it was then made a political organization, giving its support, of course, to the democratic party.'

'But is the organization connected throughout the State?'

Yes, it is. In each voting precinct there is a captain, who, in addition to his other duties, is required to make out a list of names of men in his precinct, giving all the radicals and all the democrats who are positively known, and showing also the doubtful on both sides and of both colors. This list of names is forwarded to the grand commander of the State, who is thus enabled to know who are our friends and who are not.'

'Then I suppose there would be no doubt of a conflict if the militia interfere with the people; is that your view?'

'Yes, sir; if they attempt to carry out Governor Brownlow's proclamation by shooting down Ku Klux — for he calls all southern men Ku Klux — if they go to hunting down and shooting these men, there will be war, and a bloodier one than we have ever witnessed. I have told these radicals here what they might expect in such an event. I have no powder to burn killing negroes. I intend to kill the radicals. I have told them this and more. There is not a radical leader in this town but is a marked man; and if a trouble should break out, not one of them would be left alive. I have told them that they were trying to create a disturbance and then slip out and leave the consequences to fall upon the negro; but they can't do it. Their houses are picketed, and when the fight comes not one of them would ever get out of this town alive. We don't intend they shall ever get out of the country. But I want it distinctly understood that I am opposed to any war, and will only fight in self-defence.

If the militia attack us, we will resist to the last; and, if necessary, I think I could raise 40,000 men in five days, ready for the field.'

'Do you think, general, that the Ku Klux have been of any benefit to the State?'

'No doubt of it. Since its organization the leagues have quit killing and murdering our people. There were some foolish young men who put masks on their faces and rode over the country frightening negroes; but orders have been issued to stop that, and it has ceased. You may say further that three members of the Ku Klux have been court-martialed and shot for violations of the orders not to disturb or molest people.'

'I know they (Ku Klux) are charged with many crimes they are not guilty of.'

'What do you think of negro suffrage?'

'I am opposed to it under any and all circumstances, and in our convention urged our party not to commit themselves at all upon the subject. If the negroes vote to enfranchise us, I do not think I would favor their disfranchisement. We will stand by those who help us. And here I want you to understand distinctly I am not an enemy to the negro. We want him here among us; he is the only laboring class we have; and, more than that, I would sooner trust him than the white scalawag or carpetbagger. When I entered the army I took forty-seven negroes into the army with me, and forty-five of them were surrendered with me. I said to them at the start: "This fight is against slavery; if we lose it, you

219

will be made free; if we whip the fight, and you stay with me and be good boys, I will set you free; in either case you will be free." These boys stayed with me, drove my teams, and better Confederates did not live.'

'Do you think the Ku Klux will try to intimidate the negroes at the election?'

'I do not think they will. Why, I made a speech at Brownsville the other day, and while there a lieutenant who served with me came to me and informed me that a band of radicals had been going through the country claiming to be Ku Klux, and disarming the negroes, and then selling their arms. I told him to have the matter investigated, and, if true, to have the parties arrested.'

'What do you think is the effect of the amnesty granted to your people?'

'I believe that the amnesty restored all the rights to the people, full and complete. I do not think the Federal Government has the right to disfranchise any man, but I believe that the legislatures of the States have. The objection I have to the disfranchisement in Tennessee is, that the legislature which enacted the law had no constitutional existence, and the law in itself is a nullity. Still I would respect it until changed by law. But there is a limit beyond which men can not be driven, and I am ready to die sooner than sacrifice my honor. This thing must have an end, and it is now about time for that end to come.'

'What do you think of General Grant?' I asked.

'I regard him as a great military commander, a good man, honest and liberal, and if elected will, I hope and believe, execute the laws honestly and faithfully. And by the way, a report has been published in some of the newspapers, stating that while General Grant and lady were at Corinth, in 1862, they took and carried off furniture and other property. I here brand the author as a liar. I was at Corinth only a short time ago, and I personally investigated the whole matter, talked with the people with whom he and his lady lived while here, and they say that their conduct was everything that could be expected of a gentleman and lady, and deserving the highest praise. I am opposed to General Grant in everything, but I would do him justice.' "

As soon as General Forrest read this account of the interview with him, he addressed the following letter to the correspondent who wrote it:

Memphis, September 3, 1868.
Dear Sir:

I have just read your letter in the Commercial giving a report of our conversation on Friday last. I do not think you would intentionally misrepresent me, but you have done so and, I suppose, because you mistook my meaning. The portions of your letter to which I object are corrected in the following paragraphs:

I promise the legislature my personal influence and aid in maintaining order and enforcing the laws. I have never advised the people to resist any law, but to submit to the laws, until they can be corrected by lawful legislation.

I said the militia bill would occasion no trouble, unless they violated the law by carrying out the governor's proclamation, which I believe to be unconstitutional and in violence of law, in shooting men down without trial, as recommended by that proclamation.

I said it was reported, and I believed the report, that there are forty thousand Ku Klux in Tennessee; and I believe the organization stronger in other states. I meant to imply, when I said that the Ku Klux recognize the Federal Government, that they would obey all State laws. They recognize all laws, and will obey them, so I have been informed, in protecting peaceable citizens from oppression from any quarter.

I did not say that any man's house was picketed. I did not mean to convey the idea that I would raise any troops; and, more than that, no man could do it in five days, even if they were organized.

I said that General Grant was at Holly Springs, and not at Corinth; I said the charge against him was false, but did not use the word 'liar.'

I can not consent to remain silent in this matter; for, if I did so, under an incorrect impression of my personal views, I might be looked upon as one desiring a conflict, when, in truth, I am so averse to anything of the kind that I will make any honorable sacrifice to avoid it.

Hoping that I may have this explanation placed before your readers, I remain, very respectfully,

N. B. FORREST

APPENDIX D.

The Klan Charter.

The charter of the Knights of the Ku Klux Klan granted by the Superior Court of Fulton County, Georgia, reads as follows:
"Georgia, Fulton County.

To the Superior Court of Said County:

The petition of W. J. Simmons, H. D. Shackleford, E. R. Clarkson, J. B. Frost, W. L. Smith, R. C. W. Ramspeck, G. D. Couch, L. M. Johnson, A. G. Dallas, W. E. Floding, W. C. Bennett, J. F. V. Saul, all of said State and County, respectfully shows:

1. That they desire for themselves, their associates and successors to be incorporated in the State of Georgia for the period of twenty years, with the right of renewal; when and as provided by law, as a patriotic, secret, social, benevolent order under the name and style of

'KNIGHTS OF THE KU KLUX KLAN'

2. The purpose and object of said corporation is to be purely benevolent and eleemosynary, and there shall be no capital stock or profit or gain to the members thereof.

3. The principal office and place of business shall be in Fulton County, Georgia, but petitioners desire that the corporation shall have the power to issue decrees, edicts

and certificates of organization to subordinate branches of the corporation in this or other States and elsewhere, whenever the same shall be deemed desirable in the conduct of its business.

4. The petitioners desire that the Society shall have the power to confer an initiative degree ritualism, fraternal and secret obligations, words, grip signs and ceremonies under which there shall be united only white male persons of sound health, good morals and high character; and further desire such rights, powers and privileges as are now extended to the Independent Order of Odd Fellows, Free and Accepted Masons, Knights of Pythias, *et al.*, under and by virtue of the laws of the State of Georgia.

5. Petitioners desire that there shall be a Supreme Legislative Body in which "shall be vested the power to adopt and amend constitutions and by-laws for the regulation of the general purpose and welfare of the order, and of the subordinate branches of same.

6. Petitioners desire that the 'IMPERIAL KLONVOKATION' (Supreme Legislative Body) shall be composed of the Supreme Officers and 'Kloppers' (Delegates selected by the 'Kloro' (State Convention) of the several 'Realms' (subordinate jurisdiction); and of such other persons as the constitution and by-laws of the Society may provide.

7. Petitioners desire that the business of the Society shall be under the control of the 'IMPERIAL WIZARD' (President), who shall be amenable in his official administration to the 'IMPERIAL KLONCILIUM' (Supreme

Executive Committee), a majority of whom shall have authority to act, and a two-thirds' majority power to veto the official acts of the 'IMPERIAL WIZARD' (President) in the matters pertaining to the general welfare of the Society; and to contract with other members of the Society for the purpose of promoting and conducting its interests and general welfare, in any way, manner, or method he may deem proper for the Society's progress and stability, subject to the restrictions of the power of the 'IMPERIAL WIZARD' (President) as is heretofore set forth in this paragraph.

8. Petitioners desire that they shall have the right to adopt a constitution and by-laws and elect the first KLONCILIUM (Supreme Executive Committee), which shall possess all the powers of the 'IMPERIAL KLON-VOKATION (Supreme Legislative Body) until the first organization and meeting of that body, and shall fix the number, title and terms of officers composing said 'KLONCILIUM' (Supreme Legislative Committee).

9. Petitioners desire the right to own separate unto itself and to control the sale of all paraphernalia, regalia, stationery, jewelry and such other materials needed by the subordinate branches of the order for the proper conduct of their business; the right to publish a fraternal magazine and such other literature as is needed in the conduct of the business of the order; the right to buy, hold and sell real estate and personal property suitable to the purpose of the said corporation; to sell, exchange or sublease the same or any part thereof; to mortgage or

225

create liens thereon; to borrow money and secure the payment thereof by mortgage or deed of trust and to appoint trustees in connection therewith; to execute promissory notes, to have and to use a common seal; to sue and be sued; to plead and be impleaded; to do and perform all these things and exercise all those rights, which under the laws of Georgia, are conferred upon societies or orders of like character.

10. Wherefore petitioners pray an order incorporating them, their associates and successors under the name and style aforesaid with all the powers and privileges necessary to the extension of the order or the conduct of the business and purposes of like nature."

APPENDIX E.

Application for Klan Membership.

"To His Majesty, The Imperial Wizard, Emperor of the Invisible Empire, Knights of the Ku Klux Klan (Inc.) :

I, the undersigned, a native-born, true and loyal citizen of the United States of America, being a white Gentile person of temperate habits, sound in mind, and a believer in the tenets of the Christian religion, the maintenance of white supremacy, the practice of an honorable clanishness and the principles of "pure Americanism," do voluntarily, most respectfully, seriously and unselfishly petition you for citizenship in the INVISIBLE EMPIRE, KNIGHTS OF THE KU KLUX KLAN, and to be a charter member of a Klan located at.................................State of.................

I guarantee on my honor to conform strictly to all rules and requirements regulating my "naturalization" and the continuance of my membership, and at all times a strict and loyal obedience to your constitutional authority and the constitution and laws, and all regulations and usages of the fraternity. The required "donation" accompanies this petition.

Signed ...., *Petitioner*

Date..19..............

Residence Address ....

Business Address ....

Endorsers will sign on other side.

NOTICE: Check the address to which mail may be sent."

227

APPENDIX F.

Contract Between Simmons and Clarke.

"STATE OF GEORGIA, COUNTY OF FULTON,

"This agreement, made and entered into on this the seventh day of June, A.D. 1920, by and between the Knights of the Ku Klux Klan, a corporation of said county, acting by its Imperial Wizard (President), W. J. Simmons, party of the first part, and Edward Young Clarke, of said county, party of the second part.

"Witnesseth, that the said party of the second part hereto having, by virtue of this agreement, been appointed Imperial Kleagle (General Superintendent of the organization department) of said first party, and it being desirable that the details of his rights, privileges, powers, duties, responsibilities, and compensation, etc., in addition to that laid down in the constitution and laws of the said corporation be definitely fixed:

"Therefore, it is agreed by the said parties hereto that this contract shall continue so long as it is mutually agreeable; that it shall remain of force and may be canceled by either party hereto without previous notice of any intention to do so.

"It is agreed that said second party may employ, subject to the approval and appointment of the said Imperial Wizard (President) of the corporation aforesaid, and subject to the right and power of said Imperial Wizard (President) to revoke all such appointments, such assistant organizers as he (the said second party) may deem necessary to properly carry out the plans for the propagation and extension of said corporation; provided, that such persons so appointed or employed be members of the said corporation in good and regular standing prior to their appointment, and that they maintain their good standing therein as an essential condition on which their appointment is made.

"It is agreed that in all things the second party shall be subordinate to the said Imperial Wizard (President), and shall attempt no plans or methods of work without the consent or approval of the said Imperial Wizard.

"It is agreed that the said second party shall receive as in full compensation and expenses of himself and his duly appointed and commissioned subordinate organizers the sum of $8.00 for each and every new member brought into the said corporation by himself and his assistant subordinate organizers, and in addition to the $8.00 he shall receive $2.00 for each new member added to all Klans organized by himself or his subordinate organizers within a period of six months after the date of the charter of all such Klans organized by himself and his subordinate organizers.

"It is agreed that no expense or debts shall be made or incurred by the said Edward Young Clarke or his subordinate organizers, and no obligation entered into with any firm, company, corporation, or person for which the said first party hereto or the said Imperial Wizard (President) shall be bound to make any outlay of or expenditure of money, unless there be a specific approval of the particular item or items of all such expenditures, prior to the incurring of the said corporation.

"It is agreed that the said second party shall advance, from time to time, as may be necessary the office rent and all other expenses incident to the proper conduct and furnishing of the main office of the aforesaid corporation, and in addition thereto a sum of not less than $75 per week and traveling expenses of the said Imperial Wizard (President) of the aforesaid corporation, reimbursing himself for such expenditures out of the $2.00 due to him to the aforesaid corporation on account of each member received into the aforesaid corporation by him and his duly appointed and commissioned subordinate organizers.

"Duly executed in duplicate in the city of Atlanta, Ga., on the day and date above written.

"KNIGHTS OF THE KU KLUX KLAN, INC.
"By W. J. Simmons, Imperial Wizard (President).
"Edward Young Clarke"

APPENDIX G.

Ku Klux Klan Ritual.

The name of the Ku Klux ritual is the "Kloran."

Before discussing this name, which has an interesting story, it is necessary to state that in all of the Ku Klux lingo, many words have been formed by the placing of the letter "L" after the first letter of a word. Thus we have "Klavern," the meeting place of the Klan, from "Kavern"; Kloncilium, from Koncilium; Klaliff, from Kaliff, etc., etc. The name "Kloran" is the word "Koran" with the letter "L" placed after the "K."

The "Kloran" is called the "white book," and on its front cover bears the inscription "K-Uno," from which is inferred that it is the first degree of Ku Kluxism. There is a hint in the "sacred and inspired" pages that there are other degrees to be taken, after the member has thoroughly imbibed the pages of the "Kloran," and has passed an examination upon the same. What these "higher degrees" are, no man, as far as I can learn, knows save only him, who "for fourteen years" communed with the gods and prepared himself for the sublime mission of saving the United States from nearly half of its own citizens.

231

On the inside cover is the "Ku Klux Kreed" which is borrowed from the creed of the original Klan, with such further additions as Simmons in his wisdom saw fit to add, and this is followed by the "order of business," which is similar to the average secret order, but expressed "Simmonsly" and not in the usual plain language of other organizations.

The officers of the Klan as then set forth are "The Exalted Cyclops," who corresponds to the President; the "Klaliff," to the Vice-President; "Klokard," the lecturer; "Kludd," the Chaplain (borrowed, by the way, from the name of the high priest of the ancient Druids); the "Kligrapp," the Secretary; the "Klabee," the Treasurer; the "Kladd," the conductor; the "Klarogo," the inner guard; the "Klexter," the outer guard; the "Klokann," the investigating committee; and the "Night-hawk," who has charge of candidates.

The text of the "Kloran" starts off with an "Imperial Decree" written in the "Simmons" language, and signed by "His Majesty," telling the members that the book is "the book" of the "Invisible Empire," and that the decree to preserve it, and study its sacred teachings is as binding as the original obligation. Then follows a complicated diagram of the "Klavern," or meeting-place, showing the stations of the numerous officers and the routes taken by candidates when going through the floor work.

As a matter of comparison with the original Prescript of the Old Ku Klux Klan, there are ten questions which are asked the "alien" upon his first entrance into the "outer Den" of the "Klavern." These ten questions unmistakably show an intention on the part of the "Invisible Empire" to turn the United States into a country controlled by a "class" as opposed to several "classes," and are so at variance with the requirements of the original Ku Klux Klan, as to add proof that the present organization is an historical fraud, according to its enemies, with no right to use the name of the former organization. These questions which can be found on pages 25 and 26 of the "Kloran" are as follows:

"1. Is the motive prompting your ambition to be a Klansman serious and unselfish?

"3. Are you absolutely opposed to and free of any allegiance of any nature to any cause, government, people, sect or ruler that is foreign to the United States of America?

"4. Do you believe in the tenets of the Christian religion?

"5. Do you esteem the United States of America and its institutions above any other government, civil, political or ecclesiastical, in the whole world?

"6. Will you, without mental reservation, take a solemn oath to defend, preserve and enforce same?

"7. Do you believe in clanishness and will you faithfully practice same toward Klansmen?

"8. Do you believe in and will you faithfully strive for the eternal maintenance of white supremacy?

"9. Will you faithfully obey our constitution and laws, and conform willingly to all our usages, requirements and regulations?

"10. Can you always be depended on?"

APPENDIX H.

Oath Taken By a Klansman.

The obligation, consisting of four sections, reads as follows:

"Section 1. OBEDIENCE.

"(You will say) 'I' (pronounce your full name — and repeat after me) — 'In the presence of God and man most solemnly pledge, promise, and swear, unconditionally, that I will faithfully obey the Constitution and laws; and will willingly conform to all regulations, usages, and requirements of the Knights of the Ku Klux Klan, which do now exist or which may be hereafter enacted; and will render at all times loyal respect and steadfast support to the Imperial Authority of same; and will heartily heed all official mandates, decrees, edicts, rulings, and instructions of the Imperial Wizard thereof. I will yield prompt response to all summonses, I having knowledge of same, Providence alone preventing.

"Section II. SECRECY.

"I most solemnly swear that I will forever keep sacredly secret the signs, words, and grip; and any and all other matters and knowledge of the Knights of the Ku Klux Klan, regarding which a most rigid secrecy must be maintained, which may at any time be communicated to me and will never divulge same nor even cause the same to be divulged to any person in the whole world, unless I know positively that such person is a member of this Order in good and regular standing; and not even then unless it be for the best interest of this Order.

"I most sacredly vow and most positively swear that I will not yield to bribe, flattery, threats, passion, punishment, persuasion, nor any enticements whatever coming from or offered by any person or persons, male or female for the purpose of obtaining from me a secret or secret information of the Knights of the Ku Klux Klan. I will die rather than divulge same. So help me, God. Amen!

"Section III. FIDELITY.

"(You will say) 'I' (pronounce your full name — and repeat after me) — 'Before God, and in the presence of these mysterious Klansmen, on my sacred honor, do most solemnly and sincerely pledge, promise, and swear that I will diligently guard, and faithfully foster every interest of the Knights of the Ku Klux Klan, and will maintain its social cast and dignity.

"I swear that I will not recommend any person for membership in this Order whose mind is unsound, or whose reputation I know to be bad, or whose character is doubtful or whose loyalty to our country is in any way questionable.

"I swear that I will pay promptly all just and legal demands made upon me to defray the expenses of my Klan and this Order, when same are due or called for.

"I swear that I will protect the property of the Knights of the Ku Klux Klan, of any nature whatsoever; and if any should be intrusted to my keeping, I will properly keep or rightly use same; and will freely and promptly surrender same on official demand, or if ever I am banished from or voluntarily discontinue my membership in this Order.

"I swear that I will, most determinedly, maintain peace and harmony in all the deliberations of the gatherings or assemblies of the Invisible Empire, and of any subordinate jurisdiction or Klan thereof.

"I swear that I will most strenuously discourage selfishness and selfish political ambition on the part of myself or any Klansman.

"I swear that I will never allow personal friendship, blood or family relationship, nor personal, political or professional prejudice, malice, or ill will, to influence me in casting my vote for the election or rejection of an applicant for membership in this Order, God being my Helper. Amen!

"Section IV. KLANISHNESS.

"(You will say) 'I' (pronounce your full name — and repeat after me) — 'Most solemnly pledge, promise, and swear that I will never slander, defraud, deceive, or in any manner wrong the Knights of the Ku Klux Klan, a Klansman, nor a Klansman's family, nor will I suffer the same to be done, if I can prevent it.

"I swear that I will be faithful in defending and protecting the home, reputation, and physical and business interest of a Klansman and that of a Klansman's family.

"I swear that I will at any time, without hesitating, go to the assistance or rescue of a Klansman in any way; at his call I will answer; I will be truly Klanish toward Klansmen in all things honorable.

"I swear that I will not allow any animosity, friction, nor ill will to arise and remain between myself and a Klansman; but will be constant in my efforts to promote real Klanishness among the members of this Order.

"I swear that I will keep secure to myself a secret of a Klansman when same is committed to me in the sacred bond of Klansmanship — the crime of violating this solemn oath, treason against the United States of America, rape, and malicious murder, alone excepted.

"I most solemnly assert and affirm that to the government of the United States of America and any State thereof which I may become a resident, I sacredly swear an unqualified allegiance above any other and every kind of government in the whole world. I, here and now, pledge my life, my property, my vote, and my sacred honor, to uphold its flag, its constitution, and constitutional laws; and will protect, defend, and enforce same to death.

"I swear that I will most zealously and valiantly shield and preserve, by any and all justifiable means and methods, the sacred constitutional rights and privileges of free public schools, free speech, free press, separation of church and state, liberty, white supremacy, just laws, and the pursuit of happiness, against any encroachment, of any nature, by any person or persons, political party or parties, religious sect or people, native, naturalized, or foreign of any race, color, creed, lineage, or tongue whatsoever.

"All, to which I have sworn by this oath, I will seal with my blood. Be thou my witness, Almighty God! Amen!"

APPENDIX I.

A Klan Initiation.

A Klan initiation, typical of practically all others, was held on the night of August 25, 1921, in Philadelphia, which was reported in a press telegram as follows:

"A narrow pathway leading to a woodland glade, and every fifty feet a masked and white-robed sentinel. Within the little clearing an altar, and beside it the banner of the nation with the night wind rustling through the folds. Formed in hollow square around the glade rank on rank of masked spectres. A deep voice echoing through the darkness.

" 'Imperial One, the men who seek admission to our legions stand prepared!'

"Line after line the candidates marched in, led by a gigantic masker who bore high overhead the Fiery Cross. The candidates marched before the scrutinizing ranks of silent Klansmen. Then every man — veteran Klansmen and new-made members — bowed before the American flag and through the night boomed out the watchword of the Order:

" 'All men in America must honor that flag — if we must make them honor it on their knees!'

238

"Then, in a blaze of sudden light, the Grand Goblin of the Realm, a towering form in white and scarlet uniform, appeared at the north end of the glade. Cheers received him. His speech was brief.

" 'America for real Americans!' he cried. 'Guardianship against the alien, the anarchist and all who would subvert that banner, be they white, or black or yellow!' the voice thundered through the ranks. 'The Ku Klux are misrepresented and vilified. Americans do not realize that they sleep on a red volcano's edge. They sleep; they let petty politicians hold the helm; they make no preparations for the perils yet to come. The enemies of true American principles are myriad. They are organized; they plot; they scheme — they go unchallenged and unhindered.

" 'It is the place of the Ku Klux Klan to rouse the spirit of the real American and to stand guard against the evil forces that seek to stifle this mightiest of nations. Be the foes white, black or yellow; be they native traitors or alien invaders, the Klan shall form a ring of steel to throttle their every devil's scheme. We, the Ku Klux Klan; we, the Invisible Empire, rally to aid the faltering hands of our law — and to protect our homes, our lives, our people and our nation's future against a wave of living hell!' "

239

APPENDIX J.

Klan Organization in 1921 — When the Congressional Investigation Was Held.

Acting in pursuance of the constitution, which provides that the organization is "military in character," the propagation department functions in pretty much the same manner as the army handles its business. The Imperial Kleagle is virtually a Chief of Staff, or more properly an Adjutant General. The country is divided into eight "Domains" comprising certain States, each State being shown as a "Realm," which is again divided into districts where the actual field work is done.

The "Domain" is in command of a "Grand Goblin," the "Realm" is under the jurisdiction of a "King Kleagle," while the field organizer, having charge of certain territory, is known as a "Kleagle."

The following is a list of the Domains with their respective Grand Goblins as of July 2, 1921. Of course, there have been a great many changes since 1921.

1. Domain of the Southeast, composed of Georgia, Tennessee, Virginia, Alabama, Mississippi and the two Carolinas, with M. B. Owen, Box 1472, Atlanta, as Grand Goblin.

2. Western Domain, in charge of Grand Goblin George B. Kimbro, Jr., Box 1521, Houston, Texas,

and composed of Arizona, Arkansas, Texas, Oklahoma, Louisiana, New Mexico, Colorado, Utah, Wyoming and Montana.

3. Domain of the East, Grand Goblin Lloyd P. Hooper, Apartment 1, No. 320 Central Park West, New York City, in charge, composed of the State of New York.

4. Domain of the Great Lakes, in charge of Grand Goblin C. W. Love, with headquarters in Chicago, and composed of Wisconsin, Illinois, Indiana, Kentucky, Ohio, Minnesota and Michigan.

5. Domain of the Mississippi Valley, in charge of Grand Goblin Frank A. Crippen, Box 951, St. Louis, composed of Nebraska, Missouri, Kansas, Iowa, Minnesota, South Dakota and North Dakota.

6. Domain of the Pacific Coast, in charge of Grand Goblin W. S. Coburn, No. 519 Haas Building, Los Angeles, composed of California, Washington, Nevada, Oregon and Idaho.

7. Domain of the Northwest, consolidated with former Southwestern Domain and now part of new Western Domain.

8. Capitol Domain, in charge of Grand Goblin Harry B. Terrell, Box 5, 11th Street Station, Washington, D.C., and comprising the District of Columbia.

9. Atlantic Domain, in charge of Grand Goblin F. W. Atkins, with headquarters in Philadelphia, composed of Pennsylvania, New Jersey, Delaware and Maryland.

10. New England Domain, in charge of Grand Goblin

A. J. Pardon, Jr., with headquarters in Boston, and composed of Maine, New Hampshire, Vermont, Massachusetts and Connecticut.

Unattached, Florida, to be in charge of King Kleagle S. A. Givens, who will report direct to the Imperial Kleagle and whose address is Box 1883, Jacksonville, Fla.

These "Domains" may be likened to divisions of an army, as they are in control of the spread of Ku Kluxism in the sections named, and the "Grand Goblin" reports direct to the "Imperial Kleagle." Each State or "Realm" is like a regiment, and the King Kleagle reports to his immediate chief, the "Grand Goblin," and not to the Atlanta headquarters. The "Kleagle" or field man makes his reports to the "King Kleagle" only. All communications sent to or received by him from the headquarters come through the channels of the "King Kleagle." The system is so thoroughly military that if a member of the organization writes to Atlanta about any matter, the letter is sent through channels to the Kleagle for his action.

The Kleagle is empowered to administer the obligation, organize and instruct Klans, and collect the requisite and necessary "donation" of ten dollars. Out of this sum he retains four dollars per member for his services, and at the end of the week submits a report of his activities, remitting to the King Kleagle the six dollars balance due on each member secured. The King Kleagle retains one dollar a member for his services, and remits five dollars to the Grand Goblin of the Domain to which he is attached. The Grand Goblin is allowed to shave off fifty cents a member and remits $4.50 to the Imperial Kleagle, who in turn keeps $2.50 and pays into the treasury of the Imperial Palace the sum of $2.00 which is all of the original "donation" that actually reaches the organization. The whole system is carefully conducted as a well organized sales system, each official being required to file his returns each week on a form provided for that purpose.

APPENDIX K.

Original Members of the Old Klan.

The names of the young men who met in Pulaski, Tennessee, to organize the first Klan, were Captain John C. Lester, Capt. John B. Kennedy, Captain James R. Crowe, Frank O. McCord, Richard R. Reed, and J. Calvin Jones. They were all young Confederate Army veterans.

The meeting in which they first discussed the organization of the Klan was an evening late in December, 1865. This meeting was held in the law office of Judge Thomas M. Jones, father of J. Calvin Jones. At this meeting a tentative organization was formed and from this humble beginning the Klan arose, in a few years, like a Phoenix from her ashes, to dominate the South during reconstruction times, to eventually expel the carpetbagger and the scalawag from her State governments, and to recapture for her people the rule of law and the courts.

APPENDIX L.

Judge Etheridge.

Judge Paul S. Etheridge was born March 29, 1874, in Green County, Ga., and is therefore near the Biblical three score and ten mark. He was educated in the common schools of Bartow County and graduated at Mercer University, Macon, Georgia, being admitted to the bar in 1899. He has five children, and beginning in 1918 served as commissioner of Roads and Revenues of Fulton County, Georgia, and is now a superior court judge of that county, elected in 1936. It was largely owing to his ability as an attorney that the Klan under Simmons was able to avoid many legal difficulties. He has not been general counsel for the Klan for some years. Judge Etheridge is regarded very highly in Georgia as a lawyer and a judge. He is a Mason, a Shriner, and a Baptist.

APPENDIX M.

Former Imperial Wizard Evans.

Dr. Hiram Wesley Evans was born in Ashland, Alabama, September 26, 1881. He is therefore nearly 60 years old. He graduated at the Hubbard, Texas, High School, and then studied dentistry at Vanderbilt University. He was licensed to practice dentistry in Dallas, Texas, in 1900, and followed his profession until 1920. He then became connected with the Texas Klan, and after working in that field for two years was elected Imperial Wizard and took charge of the Klan headquarters in Atlanta on December 1, 1922. He is a member of the Christian Church, a Master Mason, and the author of several books on patriotic subjects.

Dr. Evans for some time was active in national politics, at one time having a Klan headquarters in Washington, D.C., which has since been discontinued. In the 1936 campaign for governor of Georgia he was the right-hand of Governor E. D. Rivers, who was re-elected and who is reputed to be high in Klan favor and influence. Dr. Evans was rewarded for his assistance to Governor Rivers by being allowed to sell the Georgia State Highway Board a large amount of paving material, out of which he cleaned up a large sum, and which was a subject of inquiry before a Fulton County Grand Jury.

Former Imperial Wizard Evans is scheduled to go on trial in the Northern Georgia U.S. District Court in 1941, charged with using the mails with intent to defraud. He has already paid a fine of $15,000 in this Federal Court in one case. With him will be tried John W. Greer, former Georgia Purchasing Agent under the regime of Governor Ed Rivers, on similar charges.

APPENDIX N.

Statement of Rev. Caleb A. Ridley.

In the issue of August 6, 1921, the *Searchlight* printed on its first page an article by Rev. Caleb A. Ridley, a Baptist preacher of Atlanta, part of which stated:

"Some people seem to think that the Ku Klux Klan is a body of men who have banded together simply to oppose certain things they do not like — that they are anti-Jew, anti-Catholic, anti-negro, anti-foreign, anti-everything. But real Klansmen have no fight to make on any of these. I can't help being what I am racially. I am not a Jew, nor a negro, nor a foreigner. I am an Anglo-Saxon white man, so ordained by the hand and will of God, and so constituted and trained that I cannot conscientiously take either my politics or religion from some secluded ass on the other side of the world.

"Now, if somebody else is a Jew, I can't help it any more than he can. Or, if he happens to be black, I can't help that, either. If he were born under some foreign flag, I couldn't help it, and if he wants to go clear back to Italy for his religion and his politics, I cannot hinder him; but there is one thing I can do. I can object to his un-American propaganda being preached in my home or practiced in the solemn assembly of real Americans."

APPENDIX O.

Article XIV¹ of the U.S. Constitution —

(Who Are Citizens)

1. All persons born or naturalized in the United States, and subject to the jurisdiction thereof, are citizens of the United States and of the State wherein they reside. No State shall make or enforce any law which shall abridge the privileges or immunities of citizens of the United States; nor shall any State deprive any person of life, liberty, or property, without due process of law; nor deny to any person within its jurisdiction and equal protection of the laws.

(Apportionment of Representatives and the Suffrage)

2. Representatives shall be apportioned among the several States according to their respective numbers, counting the whole number of persons in each State, excluding Indians not taxed. But when the right to vote at any election for the choice of electors for President and Vice President of the United States, representatives in Congress, the executive and judicial officers of a State, or the members of the legislature thereof, is denied to any of the male inhabitants of such State, being twenty-

---

Adopted in 1868.

one years of age, and citizens of the United States, or in any way abridged, except for participation in rebellion, or other crime, the basis of representation therein shall be reduced in the proportion which the number of such male citizens shall bear to the whole number of male citizens twenty-one years of age in such State.

(Exclusion of Certain Persons from Office)

3. No person shall be a senator or representative in Congress, or elector of President and Vice President, or hold any office, civil or military, under the United States, or under any State, who, having previously taken an oath, as a member of Congress, or as an officer of the United States, or as a member of any State legislature, or as an executive or judicial officer of any State, to support the Constitution of the United States, shall have engaged in insurrection or rebellion against the same, or given aid or comfort to the enemies thereof. But Congress may by a vote of two-thirds of each House, remove such disability.

(Union and Confederate Debts)

4. The validity of the public debt of the United States, authorized by law, including debts incurred for payment of pensions and bounties for services in suppressing insurrection or rebellion, shall not be questioned. But neither the United States nor any State shall assume or pay any debt or obligation incurred in aid of insurrection or rebellion against the United States, or any claim for the loss or emancipation of any slave; but all such debts, obligations and claims shall be held illegal and void.

5. The Congress shall have power to enforce, by appropriate legislation, the provisions of this article.

APPENDIX P.

Revised and Amended Prescript of the Order of the

Ku Klux Klan in Reconstruction Days.

Damnant quod non intelligunt

APPELLATION

This Organization shall be styled and nominated, the
ORDER OF THE KU KLUX KLAN.

CREED

We, the Order of the . . . , reverentially acknowledge
the majesty and supremacy of the Divine Being, and
recognize the goodness and providence of the same. And
we recognize our relation to the United States Govern-
ment, the supremacy of the Constitution, the Constitu-
tional Laws thereof, and the Union of States thereunder.

CHARACTER AND OBJECT OF THE ORDER

This is an institution of Chivalry, Humanity, Mercy,
and Patriotism; embodying in its genius and its principles
all that is chivalric in conduct, noble in sentiment, generous in manhood, and patriotic in purpose; its peculiar
objects being,

251

First: To protect the weak, the innocent, and the defenceless, from the indignities, wrongs, and outrages of the lawless, the violent, and the brutal; to relieve the injured and oppressed; to succor the suffering and unfortunate, and especially the widows and orphans of Confederate soldiers.

Second: To protect and defend the Constitution of the United States, and all laws passed in conformity thereto, and to protect the States and the people thereof from all invasion from any source whatever.

Third: To aid and assist in the execution of all constitutional laws, and to protect the people from unlawful seizure, and from trial except by their peers in conformity to the laws of the land.

ARTICLE I
TITLES

Section 1. The officers of this Order shall consist of a Grand Wizard of the Empire, and his ten Genii; a Grand Dragon of the Realm, and his eight Hydras; a Grand Titan of the Dominion, and his six Furies; a Grand Giant of the Province, and his four Goblins; a Grand Cyclops of the Den, and his two Night-hawks; a Grand Magi, a Grand Monk, a Grand Scribe, a Grand Exchequer, a Grand Turk, and a Grand Sentinel.

Section 2. The body politic of this Order shall be known and designated as "Ghouls."

ARTICLE II
TERRITORY AND ITS DIVISIONS

Section 1. The territory embraced within the jurisdiction of this Order is:

Section 2. The Empire shall be divided into four departments, the first to be styled the Realm, and coterminous with the boundaries of the several States; the second to be styled the Dominion, and to be coterminous with such counties as the Grand Dragons of the several Realms may assign to the charge of the Grand Titan. The third to be styled the Province, and to be coterminous with the several counties; provided, the Grand Titan may, when he deems it necessary, assign two Grand Giants to one Province, prescribing, at the same time, the jurisdiction of each. The fourth department to be styled the Den, and shall embrace such part of a Province as the Grand Giant shall assign to the charge of a Grand Cyclops.

ARTICLE III

POWERS AND DUTIES OF OFFICERS

GRAND WIZARD

Section 1. The Grand Wizard, who is the supreme officer of the Empire, shall have power, and he shall be required to, appoint Grand Dragons for the different Realms of the Empire; and he shall have power to appoint his Genii, also a Grand Scribe, and a Grand Exchequer for his Department, and he shall have the sole power to issue copies of this Prescript, through his subalterns, for the organization and dissemination of the Order; and when a question of paramount importance to the interests or prosperity of the Order arises, not provided for in this Prescript, he shall have power to determine such question, and his decision shall be final until the same shall be provided for by amendment as hereinafter provided. It shall be his duty to communicate with, and receive reports from the Grand Dragons of Realms, as to the condition, strength, efficiency, and progress of the Order within their respective Realms. And it shall further be his duty to keep, by his Grand Scribe, a list of the names (without any caption or explanation whatever) of the Grand Dragons of the different Realms of the Empire, and shall number such Realms with the Arabic numerals 1, 2, 3, etc.; and he shall direct and instruct his Grand Exchequer as to the appropriation and disbursement he shall make of the revenue of the Order that comes to his hands.

GRAND DRAGON

Section 2. The Grand Dragon, who is the chief officer of the . . . shall have power, and he shall be required, to appoint a Grand Titan for each Dominion of his Realm, (not to exceed three in number for any Congressional District) said appointments being subject to the approval of the Grand Wizard of the Empire. He shall have power to appoint his Hydras; also, a Grand Scribe and a Grand Exchequer for his Department.

It shall be his duty to report to the Grand Wizard, when required by that officer, the condition, strength, efficiency, and progress of the Order within his Realm, and to transmit, through the Grand Titan, or other authorized sources, to the Order, all information, intelligence, or instruction conveyed to him by the Grand Wizard for that purpose, and all such other information or instruction as he may think will promote the interest and utility of the Order. He shall keep by his Grand Scribe, a list of the names (without caption) of the Grand Titans of the different Dominions of his Realm, and shall report the same to the Grand Wizard when required, and shall number the Dominion of his Realm with the Arabic numerals 1, 2, 3, etc. And he shall direct and instruct his Grand Exchequer as to the appropriation and disbursement he shall make of the revenue of the Order that comes to his hands.

GRAND TITAN

Section 3. The Grand Titan, who is the chief officer of the Dominion, shall have power, and he shall be required, to appoint and instruct a Grand Giant for each Province of his Dominion, such appointments, however, being subject to the approval of the Grand Dragon of the Realm. He shall have the power to appoint his Furies; also, a Grand Scribe and a Grand Exchequer for his Department. It shall be his duty to report to the Grand Dragon when required by that officer, the condition, strength, efficiency, and progress of the Order within his Dominion, and to transmit through the Grand Giant, or other authorized channels, to the Order, all information, intelligence, instruction or directions conveyed to him by the Grand Dragon for that purpose, and all such other information or instruction as he may think will enhance the interest or efficiency of the Order.

He shall keep, by his Grand Scribe, a list of the names (without caption or explanation) of the Grand Giants of the different Provinces of his Dominion, and shall report the same to the Grand Dragon when required; and shall number the Provinces of his Dominion with the

Arabic numerals 1, 2, 3, etc. And he shall direct and instruct his Grand Exchequer as to the appropriation and disbursement he shall make of the revenue of the Order that comes to his hands.

GRAND GIANT

Section 4. The Grand Giant, who is the chief officer of the Province, shall have power, and he is required, to appoint and instruct a Grand Cyclops for each Den of his Province, such appointments, however, being subject to the approval of the Grand Titan of the Dominion. And he shall have the further power to appoint his Goblins; also, a Grand Scribe and a Grand Exchequer for his Department.

It shall be his duty to supervise and administer general and special instructions in the organization and establishment of the Order within his Province, and to report to the Grand Titan, when required by that officer, the condition, strength, efficiency, and progress of the Order within his Province, and to transmit through the Grand Cyclops, or other legitimate sources, to the Order, all information, intelligence, instruction, or directions conveyed to him by the Grand Titan or other higher authority for that purpose, and all such other information or instruction as he may think would advance the purposes or prosperity of the Order. He shall keep, by his Grand Scribe, a list of the names (without caption or explanation) of the Grand Cyclops of the various Dens of his Province, and shall report the same to the Grand Titan when required; and shall number the Dens of his Province with the Arabic numerals 1, 2, 3, etc. He shall determine and limit the number of Dens to be organized and established in his Province; and he shall direct and instruct his Grand Exchequer as to the appropriation and disbursement he shall make of the revenue of the Order that comes to his hands.

GRAND CYCLOPS

Section 5. The Grand Cyclops, who is the chief officer of the Den, shall have power to appoint his Night-hawks, his Grand Scribe, his Grand Turk, his Grand Exchequer, and his Grand Sentinel. And for small offenses he may punish any member by fine, and may reprimand him for the same. And he is further empowered to admonish and reprimand his Den, or any of the members thereof, for any imprudence, irregularity, or transgression, whenever he may think that the interests, welfare, reputation or safety of the Order demand it. It shall be his duty to take charge of his Den under the instruction and with the assistance (when practicable) of the Grand Giant, and in accordance with and in conformity to the provisions of this Prescript — a copy of which shall in all cases be obtained before the formation of a Den begins. It shall further be his duty to appoint all regular meetings of his Den, and to preside at the same; to appoint irregular meetings when he deems it expedient; to preserve order and enforce discipline in his Den; to impose fines for irregularities or disobedience of orders; and to receive and initiate candidates for admission into the Order, after the same shall have been pronounced competent and worthy to become members, by the Investigating Committee herein after provided for. And it shall further be his duty to make a quarterly report to the Grand Giant of the condition, strength, efficiency, and progress of his Den, and shall communicate to the Officers and Ghouls of his Den, all information, intelligence, instruction, or direction, conveyed to him by the Grand Giant or other higher authority for that purpose; and shall from time to time administer all such other counsel, instruction or direction, as in his sound discretion, will conduce to the interests, and more effectually accomplish, the real objects and designs of the Order.

GRAND MAGI

Section 6. It shall be the duty of the Grand Magi, who is the second officer in authority of the Den, to assist the Grand Cyclops, and to obey all the orders of that officer; to preside at all meetings in the Den, in the absence of the Grand Cyclops; and to discharge during his absence all the duties and exercise all the powers and authority of that officer.

GRAND MONK

Section 7. It shall be the duty of the Grand Monk, who is the third officer in authority of the Den, to assist and obey all the orders of the Grand Cyclops and the Grand Magi; and, in the absence of both of these officers, he shall preside at and conduct the meetings in the Den, and shall discharge all the duties, and exercise all the powers and authority of the Grand Cyclops.

GRAND EXCHEQUER

Section 8. It shall be the duty of the Grand Exchequers of the different Departments to keep a correct account of all the revenue of the Order that comes to their hands, and of all paid out by them; and shall make no appropriation or disbursement of the same except under the orders and direction of the chief officer of their respective Departments. And it shall further be the duty of the Exchequers of Dens to collect the initiation fees, and all fines imposed by the Grand Cyclops, or the officer discharging his functions.

GRAND TURK

Section 9. It shall be the duty of the Grand Turk, who is the executive officer of the Grand Cyclops, to notify the Officers and Ghouls of the Den, of all informal or irregular meetings appointed by the Grand Cyclops, and to obey and execute all the orders of that officer in the control and government of his Den. It shall further be his duty to receive and question at the outposts, all candidates for admission into the Order, and shall there administer the preliminary obligation required, and then to conduct such candidate or candidates to the Grand Cyclops, and to assist him in the initiation of the same.

GRAND SCRIBE

Section 10. It shall be the duty of the Grand Scribes of the different Departments to conduct the correspondence and write the orders of the Chiefs of their Departments, when required. And it shall further be the duty of the Grand Scribes of Dens, to keep a list of the names (without any caption or explanation whatever) of the Officers and Ghouls of the Den, to call the roll at all meetings, and to make the quarterly reports under the direction and instruction of the Grand Cyclops.

GRAND SENTINEL

Section 11. It shall be the duty of the Grand Sentinel to take charge of post, and instruct the Grand Guard, under the direction and orders of the Grand Cyclops, and to relieve and dismiss the same when directed by that officer.

THE STAFF

Section 12. The Genii shall constitute the staff of the Grand Wizard; the Hydras, that of the Grand Dragon; the Furies, that of the Grand Titan; the Goblins, that of the Grand Giant; and the Night-hawks, that of the Grand Cyclops.

REMOVAL

Section 13. For any just, reasonable and substantial cause, any appointee may be removed by the authority that appointed him, and his place supplied by another appointment.

ARTICLE IV

ELECTION OF OFFICERS

Section 1. The Grand Wizard shall be elected biennially by the Grand Dragons of Realms. The first election for this office to take place on the 1st Monday in May, 1870, (a Grand Wizard having been created, by the original Prescript, to serve three years from the 1st Monday in May, 1867); all subsequent elections to take place every two years thereafter. And the incumbent Grand Wizard shall notify the Grand Dragons of the different Realms, at least six months before said election, at what time and place the same will be held; a majority vote of all the Grand Dragons present being necessary and sufficient to elect a Grand Wizard. Such election shall be by ballot, and shall be held by three Commissioners appointed by the Grand Wizard for that purpose; and in the event of a tie, the Grand Wizard shall have the casting-vote.

Section 2. The Grand Magi and the Grand Monk of Dens shall be elected annually by the Ghouls of Dens; and the first election for these officers may take place as soon as ten Ghouls have been initiated for the formation of a Den. All subsequent elections to take place every year thereafter.

Section 3. In the event of a vacancy in the office of Grand Wizard, by death, resignation, removal, or otherwise, the senior Grand Dragon of the Empire shall immediately assume and enter upon the powers and perform the duties of the Grand Wizard, and shall exercise the powers and perform the duties of said office until the same shall be filled by election; and the said senior Grand Dragon, as soon as practicable after the happening of such vacancy, shall call a convention of the Grand Dragons of Realms, to be held at such time and place as in his discretion he may deem most convenient and proper. Provided, however, that the time for assembling such Convention for the election of a Grand Wizard shall in no case exceed six months from the time such vacancy occurred; and in the event of a vacancy in any other office, the same shall immediately be filled in the manner herein before mentioned.

Section 4. The Officers heretofore elected or appointed may retain their offices during the time for which they have been so elected or appointed, at the expiration of which time and said offices shall be filled as hereinbefore provided.

ARTICLE V

JUDICIARY

Section 1. The Tribunal of Justice of this Order shall consist of a Court at the Head-quarters of the Empire, the Realm, the Dominion, the Province, and the Den, to be appointed by the Chiefs of these several Departments.

Section 2. The Court at the Head-quarters of the Empire shall consist of three Judges for the trial of Grand Dragons, and the Officers and attaches belonging to the Headquarters of the Empire.

Section 3. The Court at the Head-quarters of the Realm shall consist of theree Judges for the trial of Grand Titans, and the Officers and attaches belonging to the Head-quarters of the Realm.

Section 4. The Court at the Head-quarters of the Dominion shall consist of three Judges for the trial of Grand Giants, and the Officers and attaches belonging to the Head-quarters of the Dominion.

Section 5. The Court at the Head-quarters of the Province shall consist of five Judges for the trial of Grand Cyclops, the Grand Magis, Grand Monks, and the Grand Exchequers of Dens, and the Officers and attaches belonging to the Head-quarters of the Province.

Section 6. The Court at the Head-quarters of the Den shall consist of seven Judges appointed from the Den for the trial of Ghouls and the officers belonging to the Head-quarters of the Den.

Section 7. The Tribunal for the trial of the Grand Wizard shall be composed of at least seven Grand Dragons, to be convened by the senior Grand Dragon upon charges being preferred against the Grand Wizard; which Tribunal shall be organized and presided over by the senior Grand Dragon present; and if they find the accused guilty, they shall prescribe the penalty, and the senior Grand Dragon of the Empire shall cause the same to be executed.

Section 8. The aforesaid Courts shall summon the accused and witnesses for and against him, and if found guilty, they shall prescribe the penalty, and the Officers convening the Court shall cause the same to be executed. Provided the accused shall always have the right of appeal to the next Court above, whose decision shall be final.

Section 9. The Judges constituting the aforesaid Courts shall be selected with reference to their intelligence, integrity, and fairmindedness, and shall render their verdict without prejudice, favor, partiality, or affection, and shall be so sworn, upon the organization of the Court; and shall further be sworn to administer even-handed justice.

Section 10. The several Courts herein provided for shall be governed in their deliberations, proceedings, and judgments by the rules and regulations governing the proceedings of regular Courts-martial.

ARTICLE VI

Section 1. The revenue of this Order shall be derived as follows: For every copy of this Prescript issued to Dens, $10 will be required; $2 of which shall go into the hands of the Grand Exchequer of the Grand Giant, $2 into the hands of the Grand Exchequer of the Grand Titan, $2 into the hands of the Grand Exchequer of the Grand Dragon, and the remaining $4 into the hands of the Grand Exchequer of the Grand Wizard.

Section 2. A further source of revenue to the Empire shall be ten per cent of all the revenue of the Realms, and a tax upon Realms when the Grand Wizard shall deem it necessary and indispensable to levy the same.

Section 3. A further source of revenue to Realms shall be ten per cent of all the revenue of Dominions, and a tax upon Dominions when the Grand Dragon shall deem it necessary and indispensable to levy the same.

Section 4. A further source of revenue to Dominions shall be ten per cent of all the revenue of Provinces, and a tax upon Provinces when the Grand Giant shall deem such tax necessary and indispensable.

Section 5. A further source of revenue to Provinces shall be ten per cent of all the revenue of Dens, and a tax upon Dens when the Grand Giant shall deem such tax necessary and indispensable.

Section 6. The source of revenue to Dens shall be the initiation fees, fines, and a per capita tax, whenever the Grand Cyclops shall deem such tax necessary and indispensable to the interests and objects of the Order.

Section 7. All the revenue obtained in the manner aforesaid, shall be for the exclusive benefit of the Order, and shall be appropriated to the dissemination of the same and to the creation of a fund to meet any disbursement that it may become necessary to make to accomplish the objects of the Order and to secure the protection of the same.

ARTICLE VII

ELIGIBILITY FOR MEMBERSHIP

Section 1. No one shall be presented for admission into the Order until he shall have first been recommended by some friend or intimate who is a member, to the Investigating Committee, (which shall be composed of the Grand Cyclops, the Grand Magi, and the Grand Monk,) and who shall have investigated his antecedents and his past and present standing and connections; and after such investigation, shall have pronounced him competent and worthy to become a member. Provided, no one shall be presented for admission into, or become a member of, this Order who shall not have attained the age of eighteen years.

Section 2. No one shall become a member of this Order unless he shall voluntarily take the following oaths or obligations, and shall satisfactorily answer the following interrogatories, while kneeling, with his right hand raised to heaven, and his left hand resting on the Bible:

PRELIMINARY OBLIGATION

"I ——————— solemnly swear or affirm that I will

265

never reveal any thing that I may this day (or night) learn concerning the Order of the . . . , and that I will true answer make to such interrogatories as may be put to me touching my competency for admission into the same. So help me God."

INTERROGATORIES TO BE ASKED:

1st. Have you ever been rejected, upon application for membership in the . . . , or have you ever been expelled from the same?

2d. Are you now, or have you ever been, a member of the Radical Republican party, or either of the organizations known as the "Loyal League" and the "Grand Army of the Republic"?

3d. Are you opposed to the principles and policy of the Radical party, and to the Loyal League, and the Grand Army of the Republic, so far as you are informed of the character and purposes of those organizations?

4th. Did you belong to the Federal army during the late war, and fight against the South during the existence of the same?

5th. Are you opposed to negro equality, both social and political?

6th. Are you in favor of a white man's government in this country?

7th. Are you in favor of Constitutional liberty, and a Government of equitable laws instead of a Government of violence and oppression?

8th. Are you in favor of maintaining the Constitutional rights of the South?

9th. Are you in favor of the re-enfranchisement and

emancipation of the white men of the South, and the restiuation of theSouthern people to all their rights, alike proprietary, civil, and policital?

10th. Do you believe in the inalienable right of self-preservation of the people against the exercise of arbitrary and unlicensed power?

If the foregoing interrogatories are satisfactorily answered, and the candidate desires to go further (after something of the character and nature of the Order has thus been indicated to him) and to be admitted to the benefits, mysteries, secrets and purposes of the Order, he shall then be required to take the following final oath or obligation. But if said interrogatories are not satisfactorily answered, or the candidate declines to proceed further, he shall be discharged, after being solemnly admonished by the initiating officer of the deep secrecy to which the oath already taken has bound him, and that the extreme penalty of the law will follow a violation of the same.

Final Obligation

"I ——————— of my own free will and accord, and in the presence of Almighty God, do solemnly swear or affirm, that I will never reveal to any one not a member of the Order of the . . . , by any intimation, sign, symbol, word or act, or in any other manner whatever, any of the secrets, signs, grips, pass-words, or mysteries of the Order of the . . . , or that I am a member of the same, or that I know any one who is a member, and that I will abide by the Prescript and Edicts of the Order of the . . . So help me God."

The intiating officer will then proceed to explain to the new members the character and objects of the Order, and introduce him to the mysteries and secrets of the same; and shall read to him this Prescript and the Edicts thereof, or present the same to him for personal perusal.

ARTICLE VIII

AMENDMENTS

This prescript or any part or Edicts thereof shall never be changed, except by a two-thirds vote of the Grand Dragons of the Realms, in convention assembled, and at which convention the Grand Wizard shall preside and be entitled to a vote. And upon the application of a majority of the Grand Dragons for that purpose, the Grand Wizard shall call and appoint the time and place for said convention; which, when assembled, shall proceed to make such modifications and amendments as it may think will promote the interest, enlarge the utility, and more thoroughly effectuate the purposes of the Order.

ARTICLE IX

INTERDICTION

The origin, mysteries, and Ritual of this Order shall never be written, but the same shall be communicated orally.

ARTICLE X

EDICTS

1. No one shall become a member of a distant Den, when there is a Den established and in operation in his own immediate vicinity; nor shall any one become a member of any Den, or of this Order in any way, after he

shall have been once rejected, upon application for membership.

2. No Den, or officer, or member, or members thereof, shall operate beyond their prescribed limits, unless invited or ordered by the proper authority so to do.

3. No member shall be allowed to take any intoxicating spirits to any meeting of the Den; nor shall any member be allowed to attend a meeting while intoxicated; and for every appearance at a meeting in such condition, he shall be fined the sum of not less than one nor more than five dollars, to go into the revenue of the Order.

4. Any member may be expelled from the Order by a majority vote of the Officers and Ghouls of the Den to which he belongs; and if after such expulsion, such member shall assume any of the duties, regalia, or insignia of the Order, or in any way claim to be a member of the same, he shall be severely punished. His obligation of secrecy shall be as binding upon him after expulsion as before, and for any revelation made by him thereafter, he shall be held accountable in the same manner as if he were then a member.

.5 Upon the expulsion of any member from the Order, the Grand Cyclops, or the officer acting in his stead, shall immediately report the same to the Grand Giant of the Province, who shall cause the fact to be made known and read in each Den of his Province, and shall transmit the same, through the proper channels, to the Grand Dragon of the Realm, who shall cause it to be published to every Den in his Realm, and shall notify the Grand Dragons of contiguous Realms of the same.

6. Every Grand Cyclops shall read, or cause to be read, this Prescript and these Edicts to his Den, at least once in every month; and shall read them to each new member when he is initiated, or present the same to him for personal perusal.

7. The initiation fee of this Order shall be one dollar, to be paid when the candidate is initiated and received into the Order.

8. Dens may make such additional Edicts for their control and government as they may deem requisite and necessary. Provided, no Edict shall be made to conflict with any of the provisions or Edicts of this Prescript.

9. The most profound and rigid secrecy concerning any and everything that relates to the Order, shall at all times be maintained.

10. Any member who shall reveal or betray the secrets of this Order, shall suffer the extreme penalty of the law.

Admonition
Hush! thou art not to utter what I am; bethink thee! it was our covenant!

APPENDIX Q.

Hugo LaFayette Black, Associate Justice of the
U.S. Supreme Court.

Hugo LaFayette Black is 55 years old and a native of Clay County, Ala., where he was born February 27, 1886. He was graduated from the University of Alabama and married Josephine Foster, of Birmingham, Ala. They have three children. Justice Black began the practice of law in Birmingham in 1907, served as a police judge and prosecuting attorney and was elected to the U.S. Senate in 1927. He served one term in the Senate, 1927-33, was reelected and was in the Senate when nominated an associate justice of the U.S. Supreme Court by President Roosevelt, August, 1937.

Justice Black was one of the most prominent of the Alabama Klansmen, and Klan influence was largely responsible for his election to the U.S. Senate.

His Klan membership was brought up soon after he was nominated to the U.S. Supreme Court and some protests were filed against his nomination with the Senate Judiciary Committee, but he was confirmed without much opposition.

Justice Black is a veteran of the World War I. He entered the Officers' Training Camp at Fort Oglethorpe, Ga., August 3, 1917, was commissioned a captain of field artillery and served in the 81st Field Artillery and as adjutant in the 19th Artillery Brigade.

271

APPENDIX R.

America for Americans.

Is there a native born American whose heart does not swell with pride as he gazes upon this wonderful land that gave him birth?

Is there one, who being a son of this great land of Liberty, could owe allegiance to a foreign nation, when in his country there is peace and prosperity, where every man is equal, where his home is safe, where his children have every sort of educational advantages, where he can worship if he wants to and how he wants to, where he can enjoy life, liberty and the pursuit of happiness?

Who is the native born American whose blood does not quicken at the sight of the starry banner that prompted Francis Scott Key to write his immortal lines? Who would not give his life that this Flag which waved from Bunker Hill, from Perry's flagship, from Morro Castle and at St. Mihiel may still float supreme? Yet there are those who for a mess of pottage would sell their birthright and see this flag torn from these sockets and trampled. The Knights of The Ku Klux Klan respect other flags but bow to none but Old Glory and pledge themselves to see that it shall always float supreme, conscious of the fact that devotion to Deity, to obey and uphold the law and Constitution of our country is necessary.

No people should be as proud of their heritage, their traditions and forbears as America's Native Sons; Why? Because in their veins run the Courage of the Pilgrims, the Bravery of Boone, the Wisdom of Washington, Sagacity of Franklin, the Nobility of Lincoln and Lee. Surely the blood of kings and potentates could be no more royal — no lineage more noble. The Knights of the Ku Klux Klan desire that this blood be not polluted, but kept pure as a sacred heritage and thereby forge on to the front and take its place at the pinnacle of all nations of the world, where purity, Christianity, peace and prosperity reign supreme. This is one of the ultimate desires of the Knights of The Ku Klux Klan.

We now are the most envied of all nations. We are looked upon as a Utopia by the poor, oppressed and discontented of other lands, and to America they come and suck from her bosom her riches and at the same time maintain allegiance to their own nation. America has become more and more a melting pot, and her native born in many sections are being pushed into the background by the flood of foreigners, most of whom retain allegiance to a foreign flag.

The Knights of the Ku Klux Klan do not feel that it was for the refuse population of other lands that the Pilgrim Fathers worked and suffered to transform a "stern and rockbound coast" into a civilized country, where men might have a right to worship God in their own way.

The Knights of the Ku Klux Klan do not feel that it was for these that our forefathers overthrew foreign oppression in 1776, but feel that they suffered in the ice and snow of Valley Forge that we, her native born, might secure political independence, social security, happiness and the improvement and progress of our race.

The Knights of the Ku Klux Klan do not feel that it was for these that the train of covered wagons moved westward from the Mississippi across the prairie early in the last century, blazing an unknown trail, suffering hunger, thirst and hardships, but ever undaunted.

The Knights of the Ku Klux Klan do not feel that it was for these that our fathers welded a union of states into a great and glorious America, with their blood in 1861. When was there a war that could compare with this? No struggle has ever excelled this in fierceness, or equaled it in percentage of loss, yet none was more marked by that absence of cruelty toward the vanquished which characterized the termination of our Civil War. "Brethren of ours are these men," exclaimed the union commander, when the incomparable remnant of Lee's army surrounded by ten times their number, grounded their arms, and not a salvo of rejoicing was fired. The soldiers of Grant made haste to open their haversacks and uncork their flasks to revive and sustain the starving heroes of the South.

Compare this with the slaughter of the aristocracy of France after their revolution, the massacre of the Poles by Russia after their attempted rebellions and the bloody assizes in England.

The Knights of the Ku Klux Klan know that it was for us, their descendants, native born Americans, that our noble sires worked, struggled and fought, and it is and always will be the earnest endeavor of the Knights of the Ku Klux Klan to preserve this great Nation for its native born through Christ Jesus our Criterion of Character.

The native born American is the salt of the earth — and the ranks of the Ku Klux Klan are open only to men born in the United States.

There should be a revival of the true American spirit that made our country great and it is the aim and ambition of the Knights of the Ku Klux Klan to play a leading part in the building up of this spirit — not only in its own Legions, but among the whole American people.

The Knights of the Ku Klux Klan stand for "America First" — first in thought, first in affection, and first in the Galaxy of Nations.

The spirit of Americanism as set up by our forefathers must be preserved and cherished and kept forever alive by the burning intensity of patriotism and Christian manhood. To preserve this spirit in all its purity, integrity and perfection, The Knights of the Ku Klux Klan provide a rallying point, a guiding hand and a single aim for all true Americans.

Yesterday, today and forever — God and Government, Law and Liberty, Peace and Prosperity, America for Americans.

THE KU KLUX KREED

We, the Order of the Knights of the Ku Klux Klan, reverentially acknowledge the majesty and supremacy of the Divine Being, and recognize the goodness and providence of the same.

We recognize our relation to the Government of the United States of America, the Supremacy of its Constitution, the Union of States thereunder, and the Constitutional Laws thereof, and we shall be ever devoted to the sublime principles of a pure Americanism and valiant in the defense of its ideals and institutions.

We avow the distinction between the races of mankind as same has been decreed by the Creator, and shall ever be true in the faithful maintenance of White Supremacy and will strenuously oppose any compromise thereof in any and all things.

We appreciate the intrinsic value of a real practical fraternal relationship among men of kindred thought, purpose and ideals and the infinite benefits accruable therefrom, and shall faithfully devote ourselves to the practice of an honorable Klanishness that the life and living of each day be a constant blessing to others.

— Original Creed Revised

APPENDIX S.

A Sample Klan Proclamation.

OFFICIAL DOCUMENT — A PROCLAMATION (A-17)
To All Genii, Grand Dragons, Imperial Representatives, Hydras, Great Titans, Furies, Giants, Exalted Cyclops, Terrors and Citizens of the Invisible Empire, Greetings:

Whereas, the Knights of the Ku Klux Klan at the Tenth Imperial Klonvokation held June 5, 6 and 7, 1941, adopted a Public Americanization Program for the purpose of arousing the people of the United States to the dangers which confront our nation at home due to the activities of Communists, Nazis and Fascists, and

Whereas, Klansmen throughout the nation have displayed great interest in our program and report that they find on every side a renewed determination of Klanspeople to drive out those who are attempting to undermine Constitutional government, and

Whereas, many questions of tremendous importance to the Klan and to our nation have arisen and should have the attention of the national legislative body of the organization, and

Whereas, because the Ku Klux Klan is composed exclusively of native-born citizens it has a greater responsibility to the future of America than any other group or organization in the United States, and it must not and will not shirk that responsibility.

277

Whereas, 1942 will bring a general election at which time members of the United States Senate and Congress are to be chosen, and it is of the greatest importance that only those who place the welfare of America above every other interest be elected to the national law-making body of the United States, and

Whereas, in the normal course of events it would be 1943 before another regular Imperial Klonvocation is held, and

Whereas, I regard it as of supreme importance that the Klanspeople of the nation be assembled in the near future to map out plans for still more effective service to our country, therefore

By authority in me vested by the Constitution and Laws of the Knights of the Ku Klux Klan I, James A. Colescott, Imperial Wizard, do hereby call an Extraordinary Session of the Imperial Klonvokation, to be known as the eleventh Imperial Klonvokation of the Knights of the Ku Klux Klan to assemble in the Imperial City of Atlanta, Georgia, Thursday, March 26th, 1942, for a three-day session to take action on such matters as may properly come before the Klonvokation.

Wherefore, I have this day caused this Proclamation to be issued and have directed that the Imperial seal of the Knights of the Ku Klux Klan be affixed thereto this the third day of October in the year of our Lord nineteen hundred and forty-one, and on the Dreadful Day of the Woeful Week of the Sorrowful Month AK-LXXV.

By his lordship,

J. A. COLESCOTT
Imperial Wizard

APPENDIX T.

The Klan Today.

What Is the Klan?

The Knights of the Ku Klux Klan is the only order of men who militantly strive for the principle that all the ideals of the founders of our country should be forever supreme in America.

Who know that these ideals can be truly interpreted only by men with American racial instincts and inheritance;

Who themselves enjoy the heritage of the pioneers and recognize the solemn duty it imposes;

Who realize that human liberty is possible only under Protestant Christianity: and

Who have organized themselves for unity and the militant defense, fulfillment and enforcement of Protestantism Americanism.

It admits to its fellowship only native, white, Protestant Americans of high character.

It is secret, philosophical, non-political, benevolent and militantly operative.

It believes specifically in the following principles — America for Americans, militant Protestantism, white supremacy, militant Americanism.

Solidarity of all Protestants for social, civic and moral defense and progress.

Solidarity of all native Americans for all patriotic purposes.

Preventing social equality or political influence of any inferior race.

Complete loyalty to the U.S. Constitution.

Law and order — Just and equal laws and law enforcement, removal of the causes of lynching and mob rule, maintenance of all American rights, protection of American workers and farmers, avoidance of all foreign entanglements, restriction of immigration, prevention of any political influence by hyphenated subjects of any foreign potentate or prelate, expulsion from America of all foreign propagandists representing alien potentates or prelates.

What Has the Klan Done?

GENERAL ACHIEVEMENTS:

Brought about greater Protestant unity.

Built a national mind against Roman aggression.

Enlisted and organized a powerful army fighting incessantly for Americanism.

Built a national mind against:

Alien hyphenism — foreign entanglements — nullification of the Constitution.

Created a public sentiment for law enforcement.

Created a healthier attitude toward the public schools.

Stimulated the demand for a Federal Secretary of Education.

Aroused Americans to an understanding of anti-American propaganda, thus aiding them to a more intelligent interpretation of events and publications.

Aroused Americans to alert determination that American principles shall prevail and that American supremacy shall be maintained.

SPECIFIC ACHIEVEMENTS:

Increasing Protestant Church membership.

Maintaining separation of church and state.

Checking Romanist aggression.

Preventing a pro-Catholic war with Mexico.

Securing reservations to the World Court plan.

Securing pro-American interpretation of the Kellogg Peace Treaty.

Securing immigration restriction from 1,500,000 to 150,000 a year, with better selection.

Improving local governments.

Increasing law enforcement.

Decreasing lynchings and mobs.

Forcing Republicanism in the South to start to eliminate the blacks.

Overwhelmingly defeating Al Smith together with Tammany, corruption, alienism, nullification — and Romanism.

Why Is the Klan Needed Today?

BECAUSE:

All enemies of Protestant Americanism recognize that it is their most dangerous foe and the chief obstacle to their success. They fight us accordingly.

All enemies of Protestant Americanism are redoubling their efforts to regain everything they have lost.

All the ground we have won must be "mopped up" and consolidated.

Our successes must be pushed home to final and complete victory.

Old issues must be broadened to destroy the sources of anti-Americanism.

New specific issues and purposes have already arisen and more will arise, for the destiny of Protestant Americanism is infinite.

Eternal vigilance is the price of liberty.

Still more complete unification and coordination of all pro-American and pro-Protestant efforts is necessary.

The American spirit must be constantly aroused, informed and given leadership in a program of definite purpose.

The Klan is the only agency which has done this, is trying to do it, or is able to do it.

The aims and destiny of Protestant Americanism can be achieved only through militant organization.

The Klan is the only organization existing for this mighty purpose.

The Klan is the unifying cement of Americanism and Protestantism.

Americanism and Protestantism had relaxed their vigilance when the Klan appeared — the Klan keeps them awake.

What Is the Klan Going to Do Next?

GENERAL: Mop up! Carry on!

Develop all our successes into complete victory.

Fight for every measure that will make our country and our faith secure.

Fight for every measure that will weaken and destroy their enemies.

Fight for the complete fulfillment of Protestant Americanism.

Expose and combat all anti-American and anti-Protestant propaganda.

Educate Protestant Americans to full understanding of: white supremacy vs. Negro equality — Protestantism vs. Romanism — patriotism vs. alienism. Arouse and lead American opinion against all dangers and to the complete fulfillment of our country's divine mission.

SPECIFIC PURPOSES:

Combat Romanism in international as well as national affairs because of the Vatican State.

Prevent foreign entanglement in the World Court.

Prevent foreign entanglement and oppression from the Reparations Super-Bank.

Guard America from any loss of security through disarmament.

Reduce immigration at least by half, with more stringent regulations.

Insure adequate protection to farmers, our most American class.

Firmly establish Americanism in the Public Schools through a U.S. Department of Education.

Stop the teaching of anti-Americanism in any schools especially under the disguise of religion.

Guard America from racial degradation and political disaster by ending legalized social and political equality through repeal of the XVth Amendment.

Enact and enforce segregation and miscegenation laws.

Complete the co-ordination of all efforts for all Protestant American purposes.

Why Support the Klan?

The Klan demands of its members support in time, work, money and sacrifice. They give all gladly because they know that:

Individual liberty imposes individual responsibility on all citizens.

Consecrated civic and political service is the sacred duty of every American.

Eternal vigilance is the price of liberty not only for ourselves but for our children.

Only organized militancy can achieve any public purpose.

The Klan is the peace-time Army of Americanism, serving the nation as the United States Army does in war time.

The Klan is necessary for both Americanism and Protestantism.

For Americanism because it is the only — organization militantly striving for all patriotic purposes; organization with a definite and all-embracing patriotic program; militant army of aggressive Americanism; militant leader in the defense and fulfillment of all American ideals.

For Protestantism because it is the only — organization which co-ordinates all Protestant effort; operative organization which embraces all Protestant sects; organization able to defend Protestantism from political attack; leader for the attainment of Protestant purposes where political means are necessary.

Klansmen work, pay and sacrifice gladly because the Klan gives them the most complete, certain and effective means of serving their homes, their country and their God.

APPENDIX U.

From the Southern Trade Magazine, September, 1924,
September, 1924
Colonel Winfield Jones.

Colonel Winfield Jones, newspaperman, publicist, author, organizer and veteran soldier who contributes the splendid article on "Development of the South" in this number of Southern Trade has had an active career. He is one of the best known of the Washington correspondents. He has served for many years in the Congressional Press Gallery, representing for many years the New Orleans Picayune, San Francisco Chronicle, San Antonio Express, Manila Bulletin, Panama Journal and other great newspapers. He worked for the Hearst newspaper interests for some years and was manager of the Washington offices of the International News Service in 1911-12.

In a career of many years he filled executive positions on newspapers and magazines, including circulation, advertising, promotion, news and business management, in addition to long service as a Washington correspondent for some of the largest metropolitan newspapers in the world. For ten years he was Congressional editor of the National Tribune, the Veterans' Weekly, and when the late Frank Munsey owned the Washington Times Colonel Jones was its most brilliant editorial paragrapher.

But it is as a publicity director, publicist, organizer of great public movements that the subject of this article attained real National prominence. He is undoubtedly the most successful and experienced publicity director in this country.

His first really big propaganda work was when he became publicity director in 1913 for the American Commission on Agricultural Cooperation, a Federal Government commission, which investigated, during a tour of 14 European countries, farm banking and agricultural cooperation. The publicity resulting from this European investigation resulted in the passage by Congress of the Farm Bank Act, considered by many Congressional leaders to have been the most important legislation since the Civil War. This publicity campaign aroused the country to the necessity of agricultural banks, which at that time were unknown in the United States.

In 1916 and again in 1918 he was selected from more than 200 correspondents in the Congressional Press Gallery, which contains the ablest of the newspaper writers of this country, as publicity director of the National Republican Congressional Committee, and in 1920 was chosen to organize and direct the famous Harding and Coolidge Republican League, No. 1.

His publicity experience includes big campaigns for the National Woman's Party, the Independence Committee of Montenegro, Southern Commercial Congress, National Defense League, three pan-American governments, and many campaigns for prominent public men, including two for presidential candidates. In some of these undertakings, in addition to extraordinarily successful publicity, he raised large sums of money. The Montenegrin independence campaign was carried on not only in the United States, but in England, Italy, and the Balkan States.

During all of this strenuous work he found time to devote to authorship, beginning his literary career years ago by winning a prize in a story contest held by Short Stories, of New York, and thereafter writing many magazine articles. Three of his books, "Men in Khaki," "True Story of the Ku Klux Klan," and the "Business Man and the National Guard," achieved a wide scale. More than 600,000 copies of the National Guard publication were circulated, resulting in a big impetus for National defense legislation prior to the World War.

During his long career in Washington Colonel Jones served as secretary and later president of the National Defense League, founded in 1913 by himself and the late Representative Julius Kahn, of California, who was author of the World War selective service act; during the administration of Governor W. P. Hobby, of Texas, he was special agent for that State in Washington. The largest organization in which he participated was the formation in 1908, with G. Grosvenor Dawe, of England, of the celebrated Southern Commercial Congress, which later called the Washington conference out of which grew the organization of the now great Chamber of Commerce of the United States.

Colonel Jones conceived the idea of the Pan-American Doctrine, as an American policy superior to the Monroe Doctrine, and had this new doctrine enunciated by a foreign diplomat, Dr. Eusibio Morales, Minister of Panama to the United States, at a great conference on National defense which Colonel Jones called in Washington in 1913, this being the first conference of its kind to be held in the United States. The Pan-American Doctrine, briefly, urges a policy of "one for all and all for one" among the South and Central American republics, including the United States, each pledging support to all the others in event of war. The Monroe Doctrine does not go so far, giving all and receiving nothing, in that it merely forbids aggression of any power against any of the republics of the Western Hemisphere, and does not require the aid of any of the Pan-American nations if the United States is attacked. The late President Wilson favored the Pan-American Doctrine.

In 1897, Colonel Jones, who had then barely reached his majority, became a Southern agent for Gonzales de Quesada, head of the Cuban Revolutionary Junta in New York City, and assisted the Cuban revolutionists in their fight for freedom.

Colonel Jones served in three National Guards as an officer, in the Puerto Rican Campaign, War with Spain, and the World War. He was a colonel in the Officers' Reserve Corps, Army of the United States and is a member of many veteran and fraternal societies. He is a native of Missouri, descended from a long line of prominent Colonial and Revolutionary ancestry.

APPENDIX V.

(From the Vermont Alumni Weekly, June 6, 1936)

ALUMNI NEWS

Col. E. N. Sanctuary of New York City spoke recently in Hinesburg and Williston. He is remembered by many old-time baseball fans as a member of the "green-stocking" team that climaxed its famous career at the Chicago World's Fair in 1893. After his graduation from the University, he followed his profession of civil engineer until the World War, serving as city engineer for Montpelier; engineer in charge of construction of Bolton dam; in charge of United States river and harbor projects in the Texas-Louisiana district; engineer on construction of the Houston Ship Channel, the Galveston Grade Raising following the great tidal wave of 1900, and many other projects. He designed the dredge used in the Cape Cod cutoff and the fill at Cape May, N.J., and was president of the corporation which built the oil refinery at Texas City.

During the war he was personnel officer of military railways and in this capacity recruited the sixteen divisions of the Russian Railway Service Corps, organized under an appropriation of two million dollars by Congress for the purpose of operating the railways of Russia. His first insight into Russian Bolshevism was obtained while engaged in this service. Since that time, during a period of seventeen years, Colonel Sanctuary has not only kept in continuous contact with communism in Russia and its ramifications in this country and throughout the world, but he is a close student of all other radical "isms" through his affiliation with such research organizations as the American Vigilant Intelligence Federation which is the oldest and best informed organization in the United States on the subject of red and subversive movements. He is generally recognized as an authority in this country on communistic and other radical activities. . . His evidence is documented, authentic and reliable; he is the author of "Tainted Contacts," "Are These Things So?" and other books and numerous pamphlets."

Colonel Sanctuary is the composer of nearly five hundred religious and patriotic songs, all of which have been written, words and music, since 1936.

Press reports from Washington, Jan. 30, 1918, announced the following: "Organization of a War Service Exchange under Major E. N. Sanctuary of the Adjutant General's Department was announced today by the War Department. To this Exchange will be referred all written or oral tenders of service of any character in the army. It will be an information bureau for all applicants, and will serve as a connecting link with the Department of Labor or other agencies in search for men of special training."

From scores of letters voluntarily sent to Col. Sanctuary showing the character of service rendered his country during the World War, the two which follow pay him a well-deserved tribute: From an officer on duty with the Operations Division of the General Staff in 1921:

"I remember very well what pleasant relations I had

with you during our work together during the mobilization. I always knew that you would do everything you could to be helpful and cooperative. I am therefore writing you, asking if you will assist me a little in the preparation of an account of some of the problems of mobilization of personnel which confronted the War Department in 1917 and 1918. . . You had a very advantageous position to get a broad view of the whole situation in its larger aspects. Your work itself is an excellent proof of how clearly you realized what there was to be done in mobilizing an army of millions of men. . . My own personal knowledge of mobilization and examination into its processes makes me realize that you were intimately connected with many of the highly important operations of our mobilization, especially in questions of procurement and assignment of highly skilled technicians so badly needed in the war."

From a letter received from General McCain in 1919: "My dear Colonel:

"I left so suddenly and have been so occupied since that I have not had time to do full justice to you and others of the splendid officers who assisted me while I was head of The Adjutant General's Department, and I now wish to make such amends as I can. The work of the Adjutant General's Office, at the beginning and during the war, while I had the honor of being at its head, measured up to the highest standard of efficiency. It was never behind to any hurtful extent, and you and those under you worked efficiently and loyally, in and out of office hours, and made the administration of the office what it was. Without your assistance I could not have gotten the splendid results that were accomplished."

INDEX

292

Forrest, Gen. N. B., 26, 27, 57, 58, 66, 198, 203, 208, 209, 213, 214, 222
Forrest, Lt. Wm. M., 207
Franklin, Benj., 273
Frost, J. B., 223
Fry, Mrs. Leslie, 146

Gallivan, James A., 130, 136
Gantt, D. J., 123
Garfield, James A., 95
Garrett, Finis J., 133
Gaston, Ike, 186
George, Lloyd, 163
Givens, S. A., 242
Gordon, Gen. John B., 24, 158
Grant, Gen. U. S., 9, 67, 89, 91, 98, 158, 197, 205, 220, 221, 222
Greer, John W., 247
Gregory, Atty. Gen. Thos. W., 201

Halleck, Gen., 91
Hampton, Gen. Wade, 26
Hanks, James M., 198
Hardee, Gen. W. J., 26
Harrelson, J. Ira, 177, 181
Harris, Gov. I. G., 213, 214
Henry, Patrick, 87
Hitler, Adolf, 10
Hobby, Gov. W. P., 287
Hooper, Lloyd P., 241
Houston, Gen. Sam., 161

Jefferson, Thos., 87
Jesus Christ, 275
Johnson, Pres. Andrew, 9, 10, 11, 19, 21
Johnson, L. M., 223
Johnson, Royal C., 133
Jones, C. W., 177
Jones, J. Calvin, 244
Jones, Judge T. M., 244
Jones, Col. Winfield, 285

Kahn, Julias, 287
Kennedy, John B., 244
Key, Francis Scott, 272
Kimbro, Jr., Geo. B., 240
Knox, John, 87
Kreider, Aaron S., 133
Lanier, Sidney, 85
Lansing, Wm. E., 198
Lee, Gen. R. E., 98, 158, 273
Lester, John C., 244
Lincoln, Pres. A., 9, 10, 20, 89, 90, 104, 158, 273
Love, C. W., 241
Luther, Martin, 87, 103

Maynard, Horace, 198
McCain, Adj. Gen., 292
McCord, Frank O., 244
McReynolds, Justice, 186
Montgomery, H. C., 116
Michelson, Chas., 182
Moroles, Dr. Eusibio, 288
Morgan, Gen. John T., 209
Morton, Capt. John, 206
Morton, Senator, 197
Mosby, Gen., 91
Munsey, Frank
Mussolini, 10

Owen, M. B., 240

Page, T. Nelson, 90
Pardon, Jr., A. J., 242
Phillips, Wendell, 91
Pike, Gen. Albert, 26
Pillow, Gen. G. A., 205, 213
Pius XII, Pope, 168, 183
Poincare, 163
Poland, Luke, 198
Pool, John, 198
Porter, Gov., 212
Pou, Edw. W., 133
Pratt, Dan'l D., 198
Pulitzer, Joseph, 129

Quesada, Gonzales de

Ramspeck, R. C., 223
Reed, Richard R., 244
Rice, Benj. F., 198
Ridley, Dr. Caleb A., 126
Riordan, David J., 133
Rivers, Gov. E. D., 246, 247
Robinson, Senator J. E., 176
Rodenberg, Wm. A., 133
Roosevelt, Pres. F. D., 164 to
    184 incl.
Ryan, Thomas J., 130, 131

Sanctuary, Col. E. N., 6, 195,
    289
Saul, J. F. V., 223
Savage, F. L., 118
Schall, Thos. D., 133
Schofield, Glenni, 198
Scott, John, 198
Shackleford, H. D., 223
Sheridan, Gen., 91, 159
Sherman, Gen., 213
Shishmareff, Paquita de Louise,
    146
Simmons, Wm. J., 7, 72 to 83,
    85, 86, 108, 117, 124, 125, 127,
    135, 137 to 143, 159, 161, 165,
    192, 223, 228, 230, 232
Smith, W. L., 223
Snell, Bertrand H., 133
Spratt, H. O., 170, 173
Stalin, 10
Stanton, Edw. M., 19
Stevens, 90, 98

Stevenson, Job E., 198
Streight, Col. A. D., 205
Sumner, Chas., 12
Sumners, F. B., 170, 176 to 180
Sumners, Geo., 41
Sidney, Sir Philip, 159

Tague, Peter F., 130, 131
Talmadge, Gov. Eugene, 181
Taylor, Myron C., 182, 183
Terrill, Harry B., 241
Thomas, Roland, 134
Thorwaldsen, 158
Travis, Col. W. B., 161
Tyler, Mrs. Elizabeth, 108, 109

Upshaw, Wm. D., 131, 137

Van Deventer, Justice, 186
Van Trump, Mr., 199
Voorhees, Dan'l W., 198

Wade, Louis D., 117
Washington, Geo., 273
Weaver, Howard B., 126
Weisiger, Kendall, 194
Wetzel, Gen., 93
Wheeler, Gen., 209
Williamson, Wm., 136
Wilson, Gen. J. H., 206
Wilson, Pres. Woodrow, 65,
    166, 288
Wood, J. O., 126
Wright, C. Anderson, 130, 134

Yates, Gov. Richard, 92